C000214636

A Journey
With Brendan

Life with a child with autism,
by a mother and paediatrician

A Journey With Brendan

Life with a child with autism,
by a mother and paediatrician

Dr May Ng

Honorary Associate Professor
Consultant Paediatrician and Paediatric Endocrinologist
MBBS FRCPCH FHEA MSc LLM MBA PhD

Copyright © 2018 Dr May Ng MBBS FRCPCH FHEA MSc
LLM MBA PhD

The right of Dr May Ng MBBS FRCPCH FHEA MSc LLM
MBA PhD to be identified as the author of this work has been
asserted by her in accordance with the
Copyright, Design and Patents Act 1988.

All rights reserved. No part of this publication may be
reproduced, transmitted, or stored in a retrieval system, in any
form or by any means, without permission in writing from
the publisher, nor be otherwise circulated in
any form of binding or cover other than that in which it is
published and without
a similar condition being imposed on the subsequent
purchaser.

Typeset in Adobe Garamond

British Library Cataloguing in Publication Data.
A catalogue record for this book is available from the British
Library.

To Brendan –
You are my inspiration and you have my heart

To my mummy and papa –
Your unconditional love and encouragement has made me the person that I am today

To my son Darren and daughter Corinne –
You have my endless love; be good and kind always

To my husband Eugene –
Your love and support gives me strength

To my sister Audrey, brother Wai Tong, cousin Tien –
I cherish the times we grew up side by side and the moments we still share

To the families and children with autism –
You are not alone; patience, love and perseverance can overcome great difficulties

Endorsements

"This inspiring, highly readable book by a parent who is also a doctor and a scientist is full of useful tips for other parents of a child with autism."

Professor Simon Baron-Cohen, Director of Autism Research Centre, Cambridge University

"A mother's absorbing story of her son with autism is given perspective by her paediatric experience and medical knowledge. Dr May Ng's book will help many other affected families and also engage autism professionals."

Dame Stephanie Shirley CH DBE, entrepreneur and philanthropist (whose late son had autism)

"Dr May Ng's account of her journey as an autism mum is honest, intelligent, helpful, real-world and illuminating."

David Mitchell, bestselling author and co-translator of *The Reason I Jump* and *Fall Down 7 Times Get Up 8*

"This is a highly practical account of the difficulties faced with raising a child with autism. Despite being a paediatrician, Dr May Ng's account contains the struggles and unexpected challenges encountered in parenting; her practical advice will help others' journey through what often feels like a complex and disorientating maze"

Dr David Evans, Vice-President of Royal College of Paediatrics and Child Heath

"This inspirational book is so easy to read and is highly informative. Dr May Ng documents her personal story with autism and includes advice and information based on her experience as well as on her research and medical knowledge. Whether you are a parent, carer, employer, teacher, SENCO, relative or a friend of someone with an autistic spectrum condition, this book will certainly help you to appreciate, understand and cope."

Anna Kennedy OBE, mother and autism campaigner

"An incredible account by an outstanding mother, researcher paediatrician. The book is a gold-mine for parents and families living with autism"

Dr Udi Mahamithawa, Consultant Community Paediatrician, Autism Specialist, Lancashire

"Dr May Ng has written a must-read, full of information from her medical and personal experience describing her journey into the perilous world of parenting a child with autism"

Emeritus Professor Michael Weindling, Paediatrician, University of Liverpool

"Dr May Ng is positively masterful in sharing her personal story of living with autism from the perspective of a parent and a medical expert. Being privileged to be the Headteacher of Abbot's Lea School and working with Brendan, I can certainly confirm that the key pieces of practical useful advice offered by Dr Ng to other parents are priceless in supporting children with autism to live happy, healthy and fulfilled lives. Highly recommended and inspiring book!"

Ania Hildrey, Headteacher of Abbot's Lea School, Liverpool Specialist School for Children on the Autism Spectrum

"I wished I had a book like this when my son Alex was diagnosed with autism at the age of three. As a doctor and a mother living and breathing life with autism, Dr May Ng's book has such valuable advice and is a wealth of information for all families living with autism."

Christine Green, mother and former National Autistic Society Early Bird Programme trainer

Contents

Foreword

Autism is a lifelong disability that affects interactions with others and an individual's perception of the world. There is an impaired ability to communicate both verbally and non-verbally and this is what makes it so tough for parents. Having a child with a disability is hard for any parent, but it is particularly tough when that disability affects the ability of that child to relate in a way that a parent expects and when that disability is lifelong. And since communication between individuals is key to our humanity, that is what makes it so difficult to cope with. For a parent with a child who has such a problem, to put their feelings into writing is extremely challenging. But here is such an inspiring book. It has been written from the unique perspective of a consultant paediatrician who is also the mother of a remarkable child, Brendan, who has autism. Brendan's mother, Dr May Ng has written this book in the hope that it will help 'to clear the fog of mystery and misinformation surrounding autism'. It is a personal account of the effect that a remarkable child with autism has on an extraordinary family.

As a medical researcher, paediatrician and parent, May Ng has applied her professional skills to gain a deep understanding of what it means to have autism, its causes, current approaches to therapy and the best ways of enabling a child with autism to achieve full potential. She also gives insight into the complicated feelings of parents who have a child with autism.

Brendan is the eldest child of gifted parents. Both are extremely successful professionally, Brendan's father is an orthopaedic surgeon and his mother is a paediatric endocrinologist. The senses of pain and loss felt when Brendan's diagnosis was made were acutely felt by this family, as they would by any other. This is a moving account of a family coming to terms with the news of a diagnosis that will affect Brendan for the rest of his life.

When I first started to learn about children with autism in the 1970s, we were taught about a poorly understood condition first described by a Swiss psychiatrist Eugen Bleuler who coined the term after introducing 'schizophrenia' in 1908. He used 'autism' to describe the withdrawal from reality by people with schizophrenia. [1] Bleuler was a eugenicist and thankfully many of his ideas have not survived. It was 35 years later in 1943 that Leo Kanner usefully described autism as a distinct and separate condition [2], although the relationship between the conditions continues to be a matter of discussion [3]. There is still controversy about the causes of autism, and May Ng considers these in detail, and describes how she analysed them.

May Ng has courageously described her personal story with the intention of passing on what she has learned both as a mother and as a paediatrician with over two decades of experience of working in the National Health Service (NHS). Her story passes from the shock of discovering that her child has an incurable disability that will affect him lifelong, to a careful appraisal of the literature, which she has analysed both with the objectivity of a trained clinical scientist and the subjectivity of a parent. She recounts her battles to secure the best of care for her child, and ends with a discussion of how best to advocate for people with ASD (autistic spectrum disorder). I hope this book will encourage healthcare professionals to be advocates for families who patiently and willingly endure battles every day for the sake of their children.

This is also an account of the experiences of a family. There is a moving poem by Brendan's younger brother Darren, then aged 10: "My brother has autism / He makes me feel like a volcano / Which is just about to explode". And their mother perceptively observes that Darren has had to become Brendan's older sibling, rather than being the younger. But, as May Ng says, "There is no way round it… we had to cope with the hand we were dealt". And we can all learn from the ways this family coped: they got a dog, they went to restaurants and had to give out autism awareness cards, to Disneyland where they were embarrassed about using a disabled pass, and to a cinema, which they had to leave in the middle of the film, until they discovered several years later that autism-friendly screenings were available. These experiences, and others, have made their mother passionate about advancing autism awareness: "People, who don't judge or glare and who offer a kind word, make a world of difference".

May Ng addresses many of the challenges of child rearing, including potty training, providing general good advice. The 'Quick Tips' at the end of each chapter are practical and will help all parents, even those with children who do not have a diagnosis of autism.

This account of a family's journey with a child with autism is moving. His parents coped, because they had to. Brendan's mother writes about her love for Brendan and his needs. This is an impressive, brave and often moving account which would be a help and support to all families. I hope it will be read by all healthcare professionals, teachers and parents who are involved with children with autism.

References

1. Crespi BJ. Revisiting Bleuler: relationship between autism and schizophrenia. The British Journal of Psychiatry 2010; 96:495.
2. Kanner L. Autistic disturbances of affective contact. Nervous Child 1943; 2:217–50.
3. Crespi B, Stead P, Elliot M. Comparative genomics of autism and schizophrenia. Proc Natl Acad Sci USA 2010; 107:1736–41.

Michael Weindling
BSc MA MD FRCP FRCPCH Hon FRCA
Emeritus Professor, University of Liverpool

The Magic Box
by Darren Toh, Age 8

I will put in the box
The scent from a flower as sweet as honey
A picture of sunny Spain
And a tasty chocolate land from a faraway island

I will put in the box
The whispering winds from the calm clouds
The laughter from a smiling son
And the sound of a last note from a piano

I will put in the box
The mix of the snow and the swirling sky
The raging rivers rushing through the land
And the sound of a karaoke song in the night

I will put in the box
The gleam from a fiery firework in the sky
The trickle of honey from a jar
And a chime from a colossal clock as loud as a roar from a
dinosaur.

Introduction

I hope that this book will be my way of helping to clear the fog of mystery and misinformation surrounding autism. And in passing on my personal story I hope to include with it the best and most valuable of what I have learned along the way both as a mother and in over two decades working in the NHS as a paediatrician. I also hope it will encourage healthcare professionals to be advocates for families who patiently and willingly endure battles every day for the sake of their children.

The TV series 'The A Word' and 'The Autistic Gardener' recently brought autism into the spotlight. Today one in 60 children are believed to be on the autism spectrum. We know, from all the research and evidence, that early intervention will give the best outcome, and yet in some areas there is a 24 to 36 month wait under the NHS for diagnosis, let alone access to services, therapies and appropriate schools. The result is that many families are battling on alone, lost and desperate for help, advice and reassurance.

Ours was one of those families. My husband and I were both doctors working in the NHS, me in paediatrics and him in orthopaedics, when we had our first child. We were young, optimistic, excited – and completely unprepared for a baby who did not fit the guidelines for healthy babies, who would not eat, sleep or talk and who left us puzzled, worried and fearful.

For a long time we believed that Brendan simply had delayed speech problems and behavioural difficulties. It wasn't until he was three that he was given the diagnosis of Autistic Spectrum Disorder (ASD). Despite being a paediatrician trained in recognising the signs of autism and having my suspicions, being given the diagnosis was a huge shock and it took some time to come to terms with it.

After that we began the long journey through the wilderness of treatments, therapies, advice and red tape, and the battle for support, understanding and awareness that every parent of a child with ASD has to navigate.

Determined to do the best for my child, and in the fortunate position of being a children's doctor, I tried everything that I felt might possibly help without doing harm. And while nothing could change the diagnosis, some things did make a significant difference. I discovered that with patience and perseverance, Brendan could learn a range of skills. Over time he has learned to do many things we had been told he may never achieve. Brendan is a teenager now and we take a step each day, as long as it is a little step forward, it is progress worth cheering. The next day, you take another step and another. I don't know what the future holds for him but I know each day he is making progress with the help of his family, therapists and teachers.

No family can do this alone. We couldn't, we needed

the help of friends, doctors, therapists and teachers, and we are grateful for all that they have done, and are still doing, for us. Our hope for the future is that Brendan will lead a fulfilling life as an adult and we will be by his side, to help him along this journey.

1

The World Turned Upside Down

I stared in disbelief at the three experts sitting in front of me. What they were saying couldn't be right. Surely it couldn't?

For the past slow and painful hour, a paediatrician, a psychologist and a speech therapist had watched through a two-way mirror as I sat on the floor with my three year-old son Brendan. As I offered him different toys, tried to interest him in a game and chatted to him, Brendan ignored me and sat completely focussed on spinning the wheels of his toy car. One by one the three experts, all of them women, came in and tried to engage with him as the others continued to watch, but they had no more success than I did. As they held out toy bricks, puzzles and games and tried to engage with him, he steadfastly ignored them and refused even to make eye contact.

Increasingly anxious I tried again and again to interest

and engage him. It was beginning to feel like the longest hour of my life. Why wouldn't he play with me? Why wouldn't he make eye contact? Eventually I persuaded him to play 'row, row your boat', with me holding his hands and rocking backwards and forwards as I sang the song over and over again, trying not to sound strained. I could hear the desperation in my voice, as I forced a smile and tried to pretend we were having fun, inwardly praying that he had somehow 'passed the test', although it was quite clear that Brendan was not really having fun at all and was joining in reluctantly, only because I was holding his hands and insisting.

We were in the clinic of a child development centre in Liverpool and this assessment had come about after a speech therapist suggested it might be a good idea. Something was clearly not right with Brendan. The most significant problem was that as he approached his second birthday he still wasn't speaking – not a single meaningful word. But there were other signs of something amiss – he slept and ate poorly, and he rarely engaged with other children or adults. But because his lack of speech was the first thing anyone noticed about him I convinced myself that the only real problem was a speech delay.

I arranged for him to see a speech therapist who came to our home when he was a year old and who didn't seem overly worried about his lack of speech. She told us he probably just needed time. Relieved, I chose to believe her and waited, encouraging Brendan to speak and hoping that he was just taking his time and would suddenly, one day, come out with a whole string of words.

When that hadn't happened by the time he was eighteen months my unease once again grew and I arranged for him to see another speech therapist. This appointment, at her office, took place when he was two months past his second birthday. This speech therapist who came was highly recommended. Jane's speciality was children on the Autistic Spectrum. She was so in-demand that we had to wait many months for an appointment, which is why we didn't attend her clinic until Brendan had turned two.

Jane was warm and friendly and she spent some time with Brendan, talking to him and attempting to play with him. Brendan ignored her proffered tea set and spent several minutes crushing the head of a toy doll, as I sat watching, willing him to behave like other children, smiling, playing and joining in. He had never played with tea sets and dolls' houses and he never liked soft toys so I told myself it was too much for him to be asked to pour a cup of tea for the teddy. His lack of any imaginary play had been evident since he was a toddler.

At the end of the session Jane told me she felt she needed a second opinion from a diagnostic team. Autism is diagnosed, according to ADOS, the Autism Diagnosis Observation Schedule, by a team of three; a paediatrician, a psychologist and a speech therapist. A multi-disciplinary team is required, as the diagnosis is far from simple. I agreed, still hoping against hope that my husband Eugene and I would be told our son simply had a speech delay and that he would eventually catch up with his peers.

After the meeting with Jane, I rushed out to buy new toys, hoping that the problem had been Brendan's lack of familiarity with tea sets and dolls. Until then we had bought him 'boys' toys – trucks and trains. He had never seen a miniature tea set before. Concerned that we had been too gender-biased in what we gave him, I bought a tiny tea set, plus a few other more 'girlie' items he had ignored when Jane offered them to him – dolls with doll's hairbrushes and clothing with the intention of teaching him imaginary play such as brushing a doll's hair with a hairbrush or having a doll's tea party.

For the next few weeks I was on a mission to teach my little son how to play with these new toys appropriately. But despite my best efforts Brendan was never interested. He loved his trucks, but not because they were 'boys' toys. He didn't play imaginary games with them; he simply liked to spin their wheels, over and over and over again. In my heart of hearts I knew there was almost certainly a more serious problem than speech delay. But I could not face it. The thought that he might have a more serious or lasting condition nagged away at the back of my mind, but it was too daunting to take on board.

How could my beautiful little son have a problem? Why would he?

Once again we had a long wait for the assessment, and as the months passed I watched Brendan, hoping he would start speaking and playing with other children at his nursery. Perhaps the appointment wouldn't be necessary, I told myself. But he did not speak, and he did not play. At nursery he sat separately from the other children, spinning his truck wheels, in a world of his own.

As a result of Jane's recommendation we were invited to

attend a child development centre for the appointment with the diagnostic team a month after Brendan's third birthday. Despite all my efforts, Brendan was still not speaking, and he would not play with me or Eugene, no matter what toys we tried to tempt him with. We needed to know what was going on.

As I arrived with Brendan that day I felt anxious and full of trepidation. I hoped against hope that all would be well, that they would tell me my son was a little delayed in his speech and development, but that he would catch up.

At the end of the hour in which Brendan showed no interest at all in playing or engaging with any of us, the three experts had a brief discussion amongst themselves and then invited me to go into the observation room and join them. I did, feeling physically sick with apprehension. Their faces were hard to read, but there were no smiles. The paediatrician knew me; I had worked under her when I was training a few years earlier. Looking back it probably made breaking the news harder for her.

Once I had sat down they told me that they had agreed, unanimously, that Brendan had Autistic Spectrum Disorder and was, they believed, on the severe end of the spectrum. That was all I heard. When I look back, I am sure they said all kinds of things about therapies and management and possibly prognosis and courses I could attend, but I cannot to this day remember any of it. I was alone and all I could think was that it couldn't be true; I didn't want it to be true. They were telling me that my child had a condition that would impact our lives forever, and would make him, for the rest of his life, 'special', 'different' and reliant on care from others.

As a medical student, I had been taught how to break bad news. Our instructors told us that the patient is unlikely to retain any further information once they've been given the bad news. Now I knew how true that was. I sat nodding at the three experts, but I couldn't hear what they were saying. I have always used this experience as a reminder, when talking to my patients about difficult news and I try to give them some written information that they can look at later and to arrange to see them again soon, so that I can give them more details once the first shock has worn off. It is much easier if there is a partner or friend with them, who can support them and help them digest all the information given.

Once they had finished, I took Brendan's hand, led him out to the car and strapped him into his car seat. I felt numb. The experts' verdict, while not unexpected, was still a shock. My deepest fear had been realised.

That evening, when he got home from work, with Brendan tucked up in bed, I told Eugene the news. He sat with his head in his hands. Eugene is a contained person, not given to extremes of expression, but I could see that he was as shocked and saddened as I was.

We looked at one another.

'What do we do now?'

Neither of us had any answers on that bleak evening in September 2007. It felt as though our world, the world we had both worked so hard for, had fallen apart. Our plans for the future would change. Our working lives would change. Our hopes for our growing family – Brendan and his brother Darren, who was still a baby – would change. And we would need to learn so much. We may both have been doctors, but in this field we were as much in the dark as any other parents. But what we both knew and agreed without the need for words was that we loved our son and would not abandon him or give up on him. We would be there for him, no matter what.

My default position was to go into clinical-research mode; I decided I had to find out everything I could and discover ways to help our son. I was well aware that early intervention therapy always has a better outcome than late intervention. You can't cure autism, but you can improve the situation by starting to look for therapies and appropriate schools. So I did my best to put my feelings of shock and grief to one side and, in a state of numbness, threw myself into a fever of activity and research.

Even so, for many, many nights I lay awake and promised God that if He would only help our son to lead a normal life, I would do anything He required of me.

Quick Tips

- If you suspect that your child has ASD, see an expert as early as possible.
- For a confirmed diagnosis of ASD it requires a multi-disciplinary team, usually consisting of a paediatrician, a psychologist and a speech therapist.
- When you go to see a doctor or any other expert, take

a family member or friend along to help you remember what has been said.

- Give yourself time to absorb difficult news. Don't make any hasty decisions; allow a period of peace and calm in which to think about things and accept the situation
- Write down questions that you want to ask at the next consultation.

2

We Are a Family

When I found out that I was pregnant I was overjoyed. We had been trying for a baby for a year, so the news that I was expecting was truly welcomed.

At the time, I was a senior paediatric registrar, training in general paediatrics and specialising in paediatric endocrinology and diabetes, while my husband Eugene was a registrar training in orthopaedic surgery. We were both young and ambitious and determined to do well in our careers and both regularly working a 45-hour week. There were times, when we were both doing heavy on-calls as junior doctors, when I didn't see him for the whole weekend, from Friday night to Monday afternoon.

We had married two years earlier, in April 2002, although we had known one another since we were teenagers attending the same school in Singapore. We were both born in Malaysia, to minority Chinese families in a Muslim country, and we both won Association of Southeast Asian Nations (ASEAN) full scholarships to study in Singapore, although not at the same school. Once part of Malaysia, Singapore won independence in 1965 and despite being half the size of Wales and having no natural resources; it has become a hugely successful country and a centre of excellence. Its education system, based on the British system of O and A levels, was far better than anything Malaysia could offer. But despite this, and my pride at winning a scholarship, leaving home for boarding school in another country at the age of 14 was difficult and in the early days I was often on the phone to my parents in tears. I was very close to my parents, brother and sister and I missed them very much. They found it hard too, but they had encouraged me to try for the scholarship because they knew I would find opportunities with this education that I would be denied at home. My father had been through the deprivations of World War Two and had grown up walking barefoot for many miles to attend school, so he knew how much education meant.

Eugene had gone away to boarding school in Singapore when he was only 12 under the ASEAN scholarship. He travelled the five hours from Malaysia to Singapore alone and so he had to learn, from the start, to be resourceful and independent. Although we knew one another by sight, we didn't really get to know one another until we met in Sydney, Australia, where we both subsequently won scholarships to study medicine. I was the first Chinese Malaysian girl to be given a full scholarship in medicine from the Malaysian Government and Eugene had been the first boy. There were many scholarships for Muslim students, but not for the Chinese community at the time, which makes up less than twenty percent of the population.

I had known since I was about seven that I wanted to be a doctor working with children. When they asked me at school to write about, 'What do you want to be when you grow up?' I wrote as first choice a paediatrician and my second choice was to run a nursery. I knew at a very young age that my vocation was to look after children.

No-one in my family and generations above had ever studied medicine, not even in my extended family, and there was no pressure from my parents to do so. In fact the opposite was true; they tried to discourage me because we lived in a country where, for us as a religious minority, it was going to be difficult to get a university place to study medicine. My parents often worried that I might not be able to achieve what I wanted and so they urged me to go for something else. But I was ambitious and determined, so I pursued my dream and in Singapore I took four A levels and applied to do medicine winning a full scholarship. I was 18 when I arrived in Sydney and I was met by a friend who was already there. We looked for a house to share together and ended up in a house next to the university campus with two other girls.

Eugene was a year ahead of me, so by the time I arrived he had already done a year of the medical course. That's when we met properly. We got talking in the university book shop and he offered to carry my new medical text books to my house, which was half a mile away. Then he offered to help me prepare for my exams, showing me his notes and practice papers.

He was in a boy's dorm in the campus and he began helping me and my housemates out, carrying things back from shops for us and fixing things around the house. They all urged me to go out with him, but I wasn't sure. We were complete opposites, he was quiet, shy and studious, and I was extrovert, talkative and outgoing. He would procrastinate and I wanted things done yesterday. But he grew on me, and my room-mates kept telling me how nice he was. By the time we were halfway through our six year degrees we were a couple.

Unlike me, Eugene had been pushed into studying medicine by his family. As the eldest of four siblings in a traditional Chinese family, he was expected to achieve. His father was a headmaster and academia was held in very high esteem in the family. Eugene, while clearly very able, didn't know what he wanted to study, so his father applied for medicine for him. Eugene accepted this, and also won a full scholarship, but I'm not sure that, deep down, he really wanted to study medicine. He wasn't especially drawn to anything else either, so he stayed with medicine and did extremely well. But while I loved the idea of working with children, Eugene saw medicine as a job; he was not drawn to the 'people' side of it. He became a brilliant technical surgeon, he liked to fix things, he was extremely precise, and so surgery suited him perfectly.

We both had living expenses as part of our scholarships, but it wasn't enough money, so within months of getting to Sydney I found work as a tutor and then went on to do part-time phlebotomy, taking blood specimens from patients in hospitals, which paid much better. Eugene began doing it too and it meant we could make enough pocket money to travel around exploring Australia in our free time.

After medical school I went to Tasmania for my internship. Eugene had finished a year before me and he already had a surgical internship there. I got an internship in paediatric oncology. I did a lot of research into leukaemia and published several papers, but fairly early on I decided that children's oncology specialisation wasn't what I wanted. I couldn't cope with seeing children die and cancer in childhood was heart breaking. After three years training in Australia, we both decided to come to the UK, which offered a better training for orthopaedics and paediatrics. At that time you applied straight to an individual hospital and I was so happy when I was accepted for a job as a Senior House Officer (SHO) in paediatrics at Alder Hey Hospital in Liverpool. Eugene came with me and soon afterwards he was offered a job as a Senior House Officer at Whiston, a hospital near Alder Hey.

Although England was very different from any place we had lived before, we were very happy here. We both grew up speaking English, alongside Chinese and Malay, and within two years we both got into competitive training programmes specialising in paediatrics and orthopaedics.

By that time we were both 29, still young and in love. I had graduated in Australia at 25, and then spent two years in Tasmania, and then two as a SHO in Alder Hey. At that point we both applied for specialised registrar training, which takes a minimum of five to six years. We were accepted as trainee registrars in Merseyside, where there are eight hospitals in the area that you attend on rotation through your medical training.

We had been together for ten years, our careers were going really well and at that point we decided it was time to get married. We went back to Malaysia for the wedding; we knew that our families would be so disappointed if we didn't do it the traditional way, with each family throwing a huge Chinese wedding party.

A year later I told Eugene I wanted to try for a baby. I was 30 by then and the time felt right. Coming from a family of three siblings, I always knew I wanted three children, so I needed to get going. Eugene agreed, although I think he did so for my sake, rather than because he longed for children too. He tended to go along with my plans, swept along in the wake of my determination and enthusiasm.

After a year of trying, in which I made sure we increased our chances by using ovulation sticks which predicted when I was ovulating, I found I was pregnant. And in many ways it was a model pregnancy. I didn't smoke or have any alcohol, I took my prenatal vitamins religiously and made sure I had a healthy diet with calcium-rich food. Yes, I worked long hours, but I made sure I got to bed early when possible and that I had plenty of rest.

I was never a person who liked surprises, so at my 20 week scan we asked to know the sex of the baby and learned that we were expecting a baby boy. Happy and excited, we redecorated the guest room into a nursery room in the house and had endless conversations about where our son would go to school and university and whether he would become a doctor when he grew up. We made assumptions, as new parents-to-be do. We thought our child would be like us; hard-working, keen to learn and career-minded. It was natural that we should imagine this, as with most young parents, we just didn't imagine a child very different from ourselves.

A few years earlier we had moved into a pretty house that we renovated together, in an area where there were good schools. It was a seventeenth century, grade two listed house in Woolton, a really nice suburb of Liverpool, close to Alder Hey. We bought it because it was affordable, but it was dilapidated and it needed a lot of work doing to it. We didn't mind that as we wanted to do the work ourselves. We were happy that by improving it we could add value. Over the next two years, we renovated it from top to bottom. Because it was a Grade Two listed building, we couldn't do anything to the Georgian exterior, but inside we added new bathrooms and a kitchen, re-plastered walls and decorated. Eugene did a lot of the building work and we had professional help for some of it. We went to antique fairs and bought a lot of lovely furnishings and accessories like chandeliers, which Eugene would rewire, clean and put up himself.

The house stood in the middle of a central reservation, hidden behind trees between two big roads and when you drove either side you wouldn't even know it was there. It had a beautiful garden which we landscaped ourselves; we were in the list of Woolton's Secret Gardens every year. There was a beautiful pond which we argued over. Eugene wanted to redo it while I, with babies in mind, wanted to get rid of it. He promised to put a good safety grid over it so I agreed to keep it and he spent lots of money introducing Koi carp and other fish, but a heron ate them and every time he put in new ones, back came the greedy heron, so eventually Eugene had to give up.

It seemed that everything was in place for our family. My mother agreed to come over and help in the first few months and we finished decorating the baby's room and settled down to wait. But after an uneventful first six months, in the last third of my pregnancy I developed high blood pressure. This carries the risk of problems for both mother and baby, so it was decided that I should have a caesarean section at 38 weeks.

As the date of the birth approached, in July 2004, I became nervous, but a close friend of mine, Judith, who was a senior paediatric registrar working at the neonatal unit in the Liverpool Women's Hospital, was patiently and reassuringly waiting for me at the delivery suite.

The moment the baby was born I asked Eugene if he had all his fingers and toes. He reassured me that he did, that we had a healthy little boy and as he was crying loudly he clearly had healthy lungs too. Moments later I held him and looked at him in wonder as he lay, sleepy and warm, in the crook of my arm. Despite being born two weeks early he was a good weight – 3.19 kilos, or just over seven pounds.

I lost a lot of blood during the delivery, but I chose to take high dose iron supplements to build up my red blood cells stores, rather than having a transfusion. I was weak and tired, so breastfeeding was daunting, and in those first few days, as I attempted to nurse him in the small side-ward where we were, Brendan didn't seem able to latch on and he cried constantly. I suspected he was hungry most of the time. Rather than giving him a bottle, which would make breastfeeding harder, as the bottle is less work for the baby, the midwives suggested I cup feed him. He slurped greedily at the cup, clearly very hungry. Early birth can make breastfeeding harder, as the breasts are not yet prepared to feed, so I hoped that once we got going things would become easier. I knew all the arguments for 'breast is best' and I wanted that for him so I persevered with attempts at breastfeeding, to the point that my breasts were bleeding. But no matter how hard I tried it didn't work, Brendan just didn't seem able to latch on and suck, and we were both left exhausted and frustrated.

After a few days we were discharged and Eugene took us home. I was still recovering from the operation, so he took a few days off to be with us and my mum arrived from Malaysia to see her new grandson. I was so happy to see her, and so glad of the support and help, but the breastfeeding nightmare continued for several more days until, after a lot of tears from me and from Brendan, and days of misery in which he screamed his head off and I felt helpless, I decided to give him a bottle. He gulped greedily at it and I felt guilty for having made him go hungry.

Later, after his diagnosis, I would wonder if he had developed low blood sugar in those early days when I couldn't feed him, and if that contributed to his autism. I knew that babies with diabetic mothers can be born with low blood sugar if they're not fed very soon after birth. Of course I knew that low blood sugar does not cause autism, but my guilt at not being able to feed Brendan and my distress at his diagnosis led me to examine every moment of his life in the search for clues about what might have gone wrong and what I might have done differently.

Quick Tips

- While it's worth making every effort to breast-feed, don't push yourself or your child to the point where either of you are miserable.
- If it isn't working, ask for help or advice from your health visitor or midwife. And if it still doesn't work after every effort made, then bottle-feeding is not the end of the world. Do not feel guilty.
- Expressed milk is always an option as a way of easing the pressure to breastfeed.

3

Sleepless Nights and Food Battles

Those early days were not the calm and harmonious time I had imagined we would be having. Brendan slept very little, he cried a lot and I often felt helpless. Why wouldn't he settle at night? Why did he cry so much? I was confused, because I did everything I needed to do for him, but he wasn't contented. I felt I must be doing something wrong, but no-one could tell me what. The midwives were reassuring, telling me that some babies were just 'colicky' and he would eventually become more settled. So I could only persevere in trying to comfort him and hope they were right.

We swaddled Brendan, Chinese fashion, in a soft, lightweight muslin cloth, with his arms by his side. The idea behind this is to give the child security and comfort, recreating the closed space of the womb. Many cultures have used this practice throughout history, and certainly my mother used it for me and my brother and sister. It is believed that swaddled babies will be more settled and less fretful and will therefore sleep better.

Swaddling is only used for newborn babies in our Chinese culture, so after a few weeks we stopped swaddling Brendan. He had not been a good sleeper even when swaddled, but when we removed the wrapping we found that he was easily startled and would often wake himself up in the night. I believe that he had become too used to the feeling of being tightly swaddled and did not realise that he had arms and legs attached to his body. Being un-swaddled must have shocked him. Because of this I took the decision not to swaddle my second and third children. There is no evidence-based research on swaddling newborns.

Brendan continued to be very jittery, he was very hard to settle to sleep and he woke in the night. He slept on his back, which is the advice we give now, to reduce the risk of Sudden Infant Death Syndrome (SIDS). But he might have been happier and felt more secure on his tummy. My mother, and many others, always used to put their babies on their tummies to sleep in the past but this is not recommended now.

Eugene was very good about taking his turn looking after Brendan. I was permanently exhausted, so Eugene, who can manage on very little sleep, would get up with Brendan in the night to give me a chance to sleep.

We puzzled over why he continued to cry so much, day and night, but in the absence of any other reason we believed it was colic. Colic is the condition paediatricians diagnose when an otherwise healthy baby cries or becomes distressed frequently and for extended periods without any discernible reason. Some experts believe colic can be exacerbated by trapped wind and I tried winding him thoroughly after his feeds and then, when that failed, tried him on anti-reflux medications like Gaviscon and Infacol. However none of these seemed to help.

Studies have shown that the likelihood of having colic is lower in breastfed babies, so it was yet another reminder of my failure to successfully breastfeed Brendan when he was born. And as none of the colic remedies helped him, we simply had to persevere with our attempts to settle him and get him into a routine.

I am a great believer in routine. Babies and children need to know when things are happening and what is expected of them. They feel more secure and confident if they know adults are in charge and they know what is going to happen. So from the start we worked at getting Brendan to settle by himself. Eugene and I would take turns settling him down during the night, going in briefly to make sure that he was alright and then leaving him again. We tried, as it was often recommended, going in to settle him briefly and then leaving, and waiting five minutes before doing the same again. We didn't get him up or engage with him more than necessary, the idea was to show him that we were there and he was not alone, but at the same time to teach him that he didn't need to cry for us if he woke. It took many months, but in this way he did eventually learn to go back to sleep on his own.

Meanwhile when Brendan was six months old, in accordance with the World Health Organisation (WHO) recommendation at that time, we started to wean him. The latest research shows that babies need nothing but breast milk or baby formula milk for the first six months of life as this gives their digestive systems time to develop in order to cope with solid foods. Early weaning has been associated with development of food allergies, eczema and asthma so we didn't want to take the risk. Besides which, Brendan was perfectly happy with his bottles of milk. We had already eliminated the night feeds by giving him just water in his bottle when he woke, and although it had taken time, he was now sleeping better through the night and waking less often.

I was careful to begin the weaning process slowly with pureed organic fruits, vegetables, baby rice and porridge. It's important to give a baby the right foods, and there is quite a long list of foods to avoid at this early stage, including salt, honey, liver, shellfish and cheese. I read up on it and noted all the foods to avoid, and I made his meals myself, from fresh ingredients.

Most babies will, from the start, like some foods and dislike others, refusing or spitting out what they don't like but enjoying what they do like. But no matter what I attempted to feed him, Brendan refused it. He only wanted his formula milk and he doggedly refused to chew or open his mouth when a spoon was gently thrust towards him. I tried mixing different types of pureed food with his milk, using a cup-feeding technique, bribing him by putting a sweetener on the spoon with the food (which I knew was one of the forbidden rules in the weaning process) but to no avail.

At this point Brendan needed to start eating and learning to chew. His digestive system was ready and his body needed the variety that food would introduce. But he wasn't having any of it, and he only wanted his milk. Eugene and I were often at our wits' end as we struggled to get food into him, in between the spitting, screaming and tears. It often took us no less than an hour and a half to feed Brendan a small bowl of pureed food and it needed the two of us to manage it.

We were permanently exhausted. I have to admit that sometimes, when I was on my own, I would succumb to just letting him gleefully gulp his milk from the bottle whilst I threw away the pureed food. I didn't dare tell Eugene that I had broken the training routine but there were times when I simply couldn't face another lengthy food battle on my own.

As Brendan grew older the feeding problems continued. He was difficult to feed every step of the process – from early weaning to progression to thicker pureed foods and eventually chewing chopped solid food. But we felt we had no option but to persist because he had to eat. We would not let him get down from his seat or have his bottle of milk – which was all he really wanted – until he had finished the food on his plate.

There were times when this seemed like too big a challenge and I wondered if we were right to insist. But the alternative was that he would live on milk, which was not an option. A diet consisting only of cow's milk can result in severe iron deficiency anaemia in children as cow's milk lacks any iron. So I was determined to get Brendan onto a healthy balanced diet. And our persistence did pay off, because eventually, after many months of painstaking effort, Brendan realised that he really had no choice but to finish a meal before he had his milk bottle and got out of his chair, and by the time he was around 15 months old he began to chew his food.

Throughout that time I had the optimistic view that Brendan was just a difficult baby, but I didn't consider that there could be a serious problem. My heart used to sink at the thought of the next meal coming up and I have no doubt Eugene felt the same, but we never really talked about how big an impact Brendan had made on our lives. There were many times that I was disheartened, frustrated, angry and felt that these battles we faced with a 'difficult baby' had a human and emotional cost to our lives.

As a paediatrician, I also ensured that all of Brendan's immunisations were up to date. When he was twelve months old and it was time for the Measles Mumps Rubella (MMR) vaccine, I worried, as any parent would, about what was read in the papers and in the medical journals about the association of autism or inflammatory bowel disease with the MMR vaccine and I wondered whether he should have the single vaccines instead. One school of thought was that it was safer to give the three vaccines separately, something that was possible privately but not on the National Health Service. One of my paediatric colleagues at that time surprised me when she said that she had paid for the single vaccines at a private health clinic in Liverpool.

Was there really a risk, I wondered? I have always been active in research, so I decided to research this subject before going ahead. I looked into all the available information, I did my literature search in PubMed and Medline, read the journals, particularly from the Wakefield studies (those concerning Andrew Wakefield, the doctor who had published a research paper in 1998 alleging a link between the MMR vaccine and autism) and I firmly concluded that the advantages of the MMR protection for measles, mumps and rubella disease was crucial to my son's health. It far outweighed the unknown and unproven risks of developing autism or inflammatory bowel disease. Andrew Wakefield's research has since been discredited, but when Brendan turned one, in 2005, the arguments were still raging.

Many people chose not to vaccinate their children, believing it might result in autism, and along with other doctors I saw the results of this over the following years, when I treated un-vaccinated children with measles pneumonia and subacute sclerosing panencephalitis which is a progressive, debilitating brain disorder related to the measles infection, and a case of congenital rubella syndrome in a newborn born with blindness, deafness and heart defects because the mother was infected by Rubella infection in pregnancy and was not immunised.

I know that some parents have worried, despite the discrediting of the theory, whether having their children immunised caused their autism. But this is one area I have not worried about. I know that giving Brendan the MMR was the right thing to do, and I know too that it did not cause his autism.

- Start weaning gradually and slowly at six months old, with a variety of pureed fruits, vegetables, rice and porridge. Initially, offer the food half way through a milk feed starting with a teaspoon or two, once a day and gradually increasing.

- Your baby will learn to recognise and adapt to different textures and flavours. Try and encourage him/her to be a more adventurous eater in the future. The weaning process can be very challenging for many babies, but try not to be disheartened and persevere with the process. Seek advice from healthcare professionals.

- To encourage better sleep patterns at night when baby gets older, eliminate night feeds slowly by substituting with a bottle of water in the night and then slowly phasing it out.

- If your baby has problems accepting solid food, consult your health visitor or doctor. There are a number of possible causes for this, it doesn't necessarily indicate autism or that there is a medical problem. Weaning can often be a very challenging process.

4

Will He Ever Talk?

When Brendan was six months old I went back to work after my maternity leave. My mother came back to help us and I was so grateful – she stayed with us for the next two years and helped look after Brendan when I was at work. She went home to my father whenever Eugene or I could take annual leave, but she based herself with us for the two years and it meant that I could continue with the heavy on-call workload of a junior doctor and have peace of mind, knowing that Brendan was in the best possible hands, so I was incredibly grateful to my mother.

It's always a difficult thing combining children with a career as a hospital doctor. There is no good time to have a baby, because when you are working towards being a consultant, the training and the long hours go on for many years. If I'd waited until the end I wouldn't have had children until I was in my forties. Many doctors, understandably, choose to go part-time when they have children. But I couldn't have done that and continued towards the path that I had chosen as a paediatric endocrinologist. My work was more a vocation and has always meant a great deal to me and I didn't want to alter course at this point. I knew it would be tough, working and being a mother, but I was determined that I could do both.

By that time I was specialising in endocrinology and I had a couple of months left to complete my endocrine and diabetes specialist training. Endocrinology, which is the branch of medicine concerned with the glands and hormones, is very complex but it appealed to me very much.

Not many paediatricians specialise in this area, because it's such a specialised area and only a limited number of national trainees are needed each year. So if you want to take that direction you have to work extremely hard to be accepted for the training programme. You take the general paediatric registrar training and then, towards the end of that, you apply to a limited number of national training places into the specialised area and work towards becoming a consultant for several more years.

That was the path I was now on, training in endocrinology and diabetes at Alder Hey. I had two years of registrar training left and then another two or three years before I could become a consultant. It's called National Grid endocrine training and it is just as demanding, in terms of hours worked, as those of a junior doctor. In addition I was finishing my Master's degree in endocrinology and diabetes at Liverpool University, alongside working full-time as a registrar. A year after

Brendan's birth I won a prestigious UK Medical Research Council Fellowship grant and began work on a clinical trial and my PhD, investigating effects of thyroid and other hormones on extremely premature babies. I tailored my hours, as far as possible, to make sure that I had time with Brendan each day, and as soon as I was home I took over from my mother. Eugene and I managed the nights between us and so we all coped, but it was not an easy time.

When I first went back to work we still didn't think there was anything amiss with Brendan. He had not been an easy baby, but we had no idea that there might be anything more than that. We were sure it would all get easier as he grew bigger. But as the months passed it became clear that all was not well.

My mother was as wonderful as any grandmother could be in helping to care for her first grandchild. She constantly read and talked to Brendan even though she could see that most of the time he didn't appear to respond or to be interested. She had the difficult task of feeding him when we were at work, and she persevered patiently and lovingly, though it must have tried her patience and energy daily.

From the beginning, I documented his developmental milestones religiously. And in some areas his progress was text-book perfect. He smiled at six weeks, sat up on his own at six months, crawled at nine months and walked by eleven months. I also plotted his growth charts every month ensuring that he was growing well and appropriately, and he was. But in other areas he was slow, and as that began to emerge, we began to worry. There are basic milestones that babies need to achieve if they are developing normally. And in Brendan's case some of these milestones arrived very late, while others did not happen at all.

Most babies will begin to point by a year old, if not before. They soon learn that this is a kind of pre-verbal language in which they can indicate what they want or something that catches their attention, for example pointing at a dog in the park. But Brendan never pointed and he didn't ever make other gestures, like waving or opening his hands wide to show that his food was gone. Brendan just never attempted to communicate with us.

Babies begin to babble around three or four months old, and over the following months they form their first words, things like mama, dada, no, bye, dog, cat and so on. Brendan did start to babble, around seven months, making sounds like baba and papa, but he didn't move on to forming any sort of meaningful words.

Then there was his pincer grasp. This is the movement when a small child learns to pick something up between finger and thumb. At first, at around seven or eight months, they can only manage a spoon or a toy. But as they grow the movement becomes more refined and by a year old they can pick up something small such as a piece of a jigsaw or a sweet. Brendan's pincer grasp did develop, but it was late, around 18 months, and I was worried because I had read a study some time ago associating the age at which a child develops the pincer grasp with intelligence.

By the time he was a year old Brendan's lack of speech was very noticeable. I put this down to him being an only child with no playmates, so we started taking him to playgroup.

My mother took him two or three times a week so that he could have the stimulus of being with other children. But Brendan took no interest in the children, the songs or the activities.

We spoke to him in Chinese and English and taught him names of objects in both languages. I had researched bilingualism and the evidence showed that children who are fluent in two languages have certain cognitive advantages, such as being better at problem solving and creativity, compared to those who speak only one language.

When he was 11 months old, I bought a stack of flash cards consisting of word cards, number cards and picture cards. I was worried about his delayed speech and, coming from a Chinese culture that valued education and learning as a priority, I wanted to give him a head start in life. We began showing him the cards several times a day, something we would continue to do for the next two years. With each word, number and picture we would tell him what it was and encourage him to repeat it. But the cards seemed to mean nothing to him.

It was clear that his speech and language development was falling further behind with each month that passed. The other children at his playgroup were all talking, while Brendan was silent. I was puzzled. I knew that he was intelligent, because it would suddenly show, often in unusual ways. On many occasions, he would appear to be able to recognise the route to the local village playgroup or to the nearest McDonald's even at just 18 months old. So I put his failure to speak down to a simple speech delay.

Brendan was uninterested in most toys. He never liked

soft toys and used to throw all the cuddly toys I carefully placed in his cot onto the floor every night. He hated play dough and never tried drawing despite my numerous attempts to encourage him. I never pushed or forced him to draw or paint, hoping that he might eventually develop an interest in doing this at a later time.

While many toys and activities didn't interest him, he loved toy cars, toy trains and anything with wheels. He would throw away the little person that sat on the car, train or truck and would only be interested in the vehicle, becoming absorbed in watching the wheels turn as the vehicle moved back and forth. He did like his story books too, but they had to be read to him in exactly the same way each time, following the same order. If this didn't happen he would have a meltdown and insist we start all over again.

I should point out here that a meltdown may seem like a temper tantrum, and is often mistaken for one by the public, but it is something very different. When someone with autism has a meltdown it is an intense response to an overwhelming situation. The person loses control; they may scream, cry, kick, lash out, bite and so on, but this is the only way they can express their feeling of overwhelm until they feel safer and calmer. Getting angry with them is likely to make the situation worse as it heightens their anxieties.

Brendan's favourite books were the Thomas the Tank Engine series, but rather than reading the stories, he liked me to read him the back of these books, where there was a list of all the Thomas series books, with little pictures. He loved to guide my finger in a specific order while I named all the books.

He developed a passion for Lego and from an early age loved to make up different Lego creations, such as trucks and castles. He also loved K'nex and Meccano, transportation building sets, and he spent hours playing with them. And we discovered that he was a natural born swimmer. When he was two we visited Center Parcs and took him into the swimming pool and he loved it. Happy and at ease in his armbands, he splashed and floated around, clearly enjoying himself.

This was in marked contrast to his visits to parks and playgrounds. We often took him, but he was never interested in playing with the swings or slides; he usually preferred to concentrate on feeling the ground or the grass for minutes at a time. And if there were other children around, he took no notice of them.

As boys often speak later than girls we decided to wait before taking action, but when Brendan was almost two years old and still not speaking a single recognisable word, I became increasingly worried and referred him for a hearing test and a speech assessment. It was in my mind merely precautionary at that time and it had never occurred to me that he may have a medical diagnosis. I relied on my clinical experience and reassured myself that it was most likely a temporary speech delay, possibly arising from our speaking two languages at home. While there are clear advantages for a child in growing up bilingual, there are speech therapists we met who claim that using dual languages at a young age can cause temporary speech delay and language disorders. They claim that hearing two languages may confuse the child and lead to problems in acquiring expressive or receptive language and in this situation they say that it's better to stick to one language in the home environment. There is no substantive scientific evidence to date that states using two languages leads to speech delays or disorders in language acquisition, this theory is simply a view taken by some speech therapists whom we met.

Brendan's hearing assessment was normal. His speech and language assessment took place when he was 26 months old due to an extremely long waiting list in the area that we were living in. The first visit was at the clinic where the speech therapist showed him several toys which included a teddy, a bed, a tea set and a comb. Brendan did not seem to know what to do with the items but he did eventually take the comb when prompted and combed his own hair. I was told at the time by the speech therapist that he needed to be assessed again by a joint team consisting of a paediatrician, a speech therapist and a psychologist at the Joint Assessment Clinic in a few months' time as she was not able to make a conclusive diagnosis. I was also told at the time that we should stick to using a mono-language environment for Brendan until further assessments.

I convinced myself that he was probably fine, and that his failure to play with some of the toys, when prompted by the therapist, had been because he had never played with them before. He didn't know what to do with a tea set or a doll's house. After the assessment I rushed out to buy them for him. I was on a mission to teach him how to 'pass the test', determined that when we got to the Joint Assessment Clinic he would perform perfectly.

- If you are a bilingual household, don't be afraid to teach your child two languages from the beginning. For most children this is an advantage and it should only be stopped on the advice of a qualified speech therapist.
- Never be afraid to ask for a second opinion about any of your child's health issues if there are questions left unanswered.
- Delayed speech is common in children but if you have ongoing concerns, ask for a referral to a speech and language specialist.
- It is important to keep in mind that there are average time frames for achieving developmental milestones and some children may achieve various developmental milestones earlier or later than the average but still be within the normal range.

5

Acceptance

The day Brendan had his assessment and diagnosis remains vivid for me because that day our lives changed. It was a turning point, and nothing would ever be quite the same again. It was the summer of 2007 and he was exactly three years and one month old.

On my way home I was still in denial, convinced that these three highly-experienced health professionals must have got it wrong. Surely it was a simple speech delay and Brendan would grow out of his strange attitudes and difficult behaviours?

I got through the day like a zombie, waiting for Eugene to come home. When he did, I broke the news to him and by the end of the evening we were both in tears.

The 'why me?' questions kept popping into my head. By then, I was on my way to becoming a Consultant Paediatrician with dual specialist accreditation in Paediatrics and Paediatric Endocrinology and Diabetes. I had completed my Master of Medical Science degree and was now working on my PhD degree. Eugene was equally driven and hard-working training in Orthopaedics and Trauma surgery. With hindsight it might sound a little naive to say it, since any two parents can have a child with autism, no matter what their background or ability, but at the time we could only feel stunned. How could our son have this diagnosis? Not only were we both high-achieving, but neither of us had any family history of autism and I had done everything by the book during my pregnancy.

Despite this I was convinced, for a very long time, that I had done something to cause Brendan's autism. My guilt was all consuming and I examined, in minute detail, everything I had done, or eaten or taken; trying to find the key to what had gone wrong.

I shuttled between being angry and becoming depressed. I couldn't sleep, I would spend all night praying and bargaining with God, promising that if He made Brendan normal I would never ask for anything else, I would make everyone go to church, I would do good deeds for society for the rest of my life. It wasn't fair, I didn't deserve this. How could it have happened? I simply could not face dealing with the diagnosis and what it entailed. As a paediatrician I had often seen patients with autism and I knew only too well the demands and challenges that caring for these children entailed for their parents.

Within weeks I was overcome by a deep sense of grief. I would sit staring at my son intently as he examined, for the hundredth time that day, the rotating wheels of his toy truck, grieving for the loss of the son that I could have had. I could not eat or sleep.

I went through the motions of life – going to work, coming home and looking after Brendan and Darren, studying, going to bed, getting up again. But I was numb, simply functioning while inwardly consumed by bewilderment and grief.

No-one at work knew what I was going through in my personal life. Perhaps I should have told someone, but it simply felt too hard to tell my work colleagues about something which felt so overwhelming and heart breaking that it was consuming me.

I questioned everything. Had I been right to have a child at all? And then to have a second one, when the first showed signs of problems?

Darren, our second son, had been born just before Brendan turned two. And I had been so happy to have our two boys, planned to be close in age so that they could be friends and companions. I pictured them supporting and helping one another in their lives, as children and as adults. But with the diagnosis that picture had changed dramatically. What kind of a burden might Brendan's diagnosis be for Darren? And was Darren a healthy child?

I had always wanted two or three children and for them to be close in age so that they would grow up together, with a strong bond. And although Brendan was a difficult baby, I had been optimistic, believing that he would grow out of his problems. So by the time Brendan was 15 months old I had conceived again.

Looking back I know that Eugene and I didn't talk

enough about all the issues in our lives. We went to work, came home and cared for Brendan and that occupied most of our life at that time. We didn't really discuss having another child – it was my plan, and Eugene went along with it. For me children were so important and he knew that and put aside his own feelings and wishes. Another child meant less time for him, greater expense and a lot of night time work and, as I discovered much later, he had doubts about the wisdom of it, but he did not say so.

In 2006, while I was pregnant with Darren, I received a very prestigious medical research fellowship grant for a minimum of three years. This meant that I would receive a full salary for running a research trial into the effects of thyroxine and other endocrine hormones in very premature babies. This trial ran in hospitals across the country and I was given the task of coordinating and managing the trial in all clinical aspects. This was a challenge, but at the same time working on the research trial meant that I could do some of my work from home and at the same time work on my PhD thesis. It fitted very well with having children, and the flexibility allowed me to spend more time with them and at the same time to enjoy the academic work. I also had the most wonderful supervisor who till today remains my mentor and lifelong friend.

My pregnancy with Darren was not straightforward – in the second half I developed hypertension (high blood pressure) which meant that I had to be carefully monitored. Hypertension can lead to disorders which put both mother and baby at risk. The foremost risk is of pre-eclampsia, a potentially dangerous condition in which the flow of blood through the placenta is reduced, so that the baby does not receive enough oxygen and nutrients. This often leads to premature birth, because pre-eclampsia can only be resolved by the birth of the baby.

In addition it was discovered that I was presented with Placenta Praevia, in which the placenta sits across the entrance to the womb, blocking the outlet. This carries additional risks and makes a natural birth impossible; I would need another caesarean, and in view of my condition, this was planned for 34 weeks.

The birth was difficult; I lost a lot of blood and was in intensive care for three days. I needed a blood transfusion and was unable to feed Darren. He was with me, and was given bottle feeds, although when I was well enough I did express breastmilk for him.

By the time I came home from hospital with Darren, my mother had been with us for two years. And while she never complained, I knew she had sacrificed a lot to help us. In Malaysia she was able to be independent, she had plenty of friends and, of course, she was with my father. In the UK she couldn't drive and she didn't have friends, so it must have been very lonely for her.

Two months after Darren's birth my younger sister had her first baby in Malaysia, a son named James. It was time for my mother to go home, to help my sister as she had helped me, and to resume her life. I was hugely grateful for all she had done and after she had left we missed her deeply – not just for her help, but for her warm and supportive company.

At this point I had a newborn baby and a challenging

two year-old and I was working on my clinical trial, juggling my time and doing as much work as I could from home. Eugene was working full-time, so for most of the day I was coping on my own. We needed help, so we decided to hire a live-in au pair. That was a help, but it was a tough time. Eugene was distant and lonely and I was hyper-stressed and volatile. We had no time to ourselves and no energy for one another.

From the start we put Darren in with Brendan at night. We thought that sharing a room might be good for both of them. So Darren's Moses basket sat beside Brendan's bed. Brendan completely ignored him; it was as though his baby brother simply wasn't there. Darren was too young to mind, he simply slept, although when Brendan woke, as he still did several times every night, he also often woke Darren.

By the time the autism diagnosis was made, Darren was a year old. He had always been an easy baby. He slept well, he smiled often and responded to us and when the time came to wean him at six months old, he made the transition to solids without any problems. I was relieved and grateful.

Meanwhile Brendan remained in his own little world. He didn't like to be cuddled or hugged and he spent most of his time absorbed with his favourite toys – the trucks with the spinning wheels and his Lego.

At mealtimes he continued to be a very reluctant and fussy eater, insisting that different foods were separated on his plate and that there were no 'messy' sauces or gravy. It still took a lot of time to get through a meal with him and often left us frustrated and tired.

He still was not speaking and I wondered whether

he ever would. I persisted in working with him; trying everything I could to encourage him. But all too often my efforts were met with blank disinterest and all I felt was despair and fear for the future – his and ours.

Then one evening I, after another exhausting session going through the motions of making Brendan look and listen to the stack of flashcards that I would flash in front of him each night, I carried him to his cot and gave him a goodnight kiss. All of a sudden Brendan looked up into my eyes, smiled and said 'mama'. I was stunned. He rarely made eye contact and had never said 'mama' before.

As I looked down at him something inside me – the knot of angst and distress, anger and grief – dissolved. I felt in my heart that he was trying to tell me 'Mummy, it's alright. I love you'. Whether he had sensed my sadness, I will never know, but that moment jolted me out of my self-pity and all I felt was love. That was the day I accepted Brendan for who he was and knew that I had to be his mother, to love him unconditionally and to help him in every way I could.

Quick Tips

- However tough things get, make a little time for your partner, if you have one. You're in this together and if you are kind to one another and you keep the communication channels open you can help and support one another.
- Sometimes, the cycle of denial, anger, depression,

bargaining, and acceptance is simply unavoidable and talking to a trusted other or counselling can help.

- Ask family members for help to give you and your partner some respite time away from the children.
- Small children can feel comforted and safer sharing a room with their siblings.

6

Potty Training

This subject, simple as it seems, can be anything but, and as it is so very important and so often underrated, I feel it deserves a chapter on its own. A surprising number of children are not potty trained, with enormous consequences for them and their parents. Teaching potty training, as we learned in our own case, requires a high degree of dedication, perseverance and determination.

The current advice says that you should begin to potty train a child from around the age of three, and this is what we did with Brendan at just under three years old, encouraging him to sit on his potty several times a day, in order to make the transition from nappies to using a toilet.

As a paediatrician I see a lot of children who are not fully potty trained at a much older age than three. I also see a lot of children who are constipated. So in addition to teaching Brendan to use the toilet, we also wanted to teach him to open his bowels every day, a habit that would stand him in good stead for life.

Potty training was probably one of our biggest challenges. If we had thought that feeding Brendan was difficult, then this was twice as bad. Brendan was as determined not to use the potty as we were to get him to use it. And so the battle of wills raged. But this was one I was absolutely determined to win. I was not willing to have a child, whatever his condition, or not, who could not take himself to the toilet and use it. And so we persevered.

Each day several hours were spent with Brendan sitting on his plastic toilet seat and me, or Eugene, sitting in the bathroom with him, encouraging him to wee or poo. But Brendan simply hated being anywhere near the toilet; he didn't even like to stand beside it, let alone sit on it.

It was only later that I realised he was distressed by the sound of the water flushing because of his sensory processing disorder (SPD). This is a condition that can be separate to autism, some children have one and not the other, but often the two go hand-in-hand. With SPD the brain has trouble organising information from the senses. Children with this disorder can be highly sensitive to sights, sounds, textures, flavours and smells (more on this in chapter 13).

In Brendan's case the sound of the toilet flush and water running in the cistern distressed him so much that he would scream and throw himself on the ground. And he refused, point blank, to do anything at all while sitting on the toilet. Then the minute we let him off, he would wee or poo in his pants. At times he would smear faeces on the walls and the furniture because he had dirtied his pants and was trying to get rid of the poo.

We tried everything we could think of. We held him on the toilet, sometimes for a minute or two, sometimes for up to half an hour. Nothing. We distracted him with his favourite television programme (yes – we actually brought the TV into the bathroom) and by letting him play with his favourite toys while he was sitting on the toilet. But none of it had any effect. Showing an impressive degree of bladder and bowel control, Brendan would hang on until, exhausted and out of ideas, we finally let him off the toilet – when he would perform on the floor, in his pants or on the furniture. We could only scold him, so that he would understand this was wrong, and then clean up after him.

The ordeal went on for months and at times we despaired. Ideally a child should be fully potty trained by the age of four. And I, more than most, knew the consequences if this did not happen. I regularly see children of six, seven, eight and older still in nappies, with parents resigned to having to change nappies on their growing youngsters for the foreseeable future. And yet, for many such children, this does not need to be the case. Of course there are those with medical conditions that mean they will never be able to use a toilet independently. But many of the children I see have gone through all kinds of medical investigations and interventions, when in fact the problem is that they have simply not been potty trained with a routine.

I believe it is absolutely possible to potty train most children, even those with autism, learning difficulties and a number of other conditions. Once they are potty trained it gives them a vital degree of independence and self-regard. And of course the relief (quite literally) for the parents is enormous. But it takes a great deal of time, effort and persistence – in some cases so much so that parents give up, believing it will never happen.

Even with this knowledge, it was difficult to keep going with Brendan. For day after day, month after month, we took him to the toilet, sitting him there and then watching him get down and, often within moments, soil his clothing.

When we first began the potty training we didn't have the autism diagnosis. But knowing that he had autism didn't really help, other than to alert us to the fact that it would perhaps be more difficult. We still needed to teach him to use a toilet. He would need to do this daily for the rest of his life, we would not always be there to change nappies. Growing up without being taught to use the toilet was simply, for us, not an option. He needed to learn – but how do we teach him?

It was as if he simply did not understand what he was meant to do, despite our huge efforts to show him and to explain. We used laminated cards with pictures, stuck on the bathroom wall, we used rewards and we persisted despite his wails of protest.

The ordeal went on for eleven months. We dreaded potty time even more than meal time. Thankfully there were two of us to take turns. Repetition was the key; there was simply no short-cut to achieving the goal. We always gave him lots of praise if he should happen to go in the toilet and we had a potty star chart with a picture of a boy on a potty. It was rare for him to earn a star, but we kept on encouraging him and insisting he sit on the toilet.

Then one day Brendan, quite suddenly, seemed to realise what he was meant to do. He accepted the toilet as part of his routine, and today, he opens his bowels regularly daily and has rarely had an accident since. It changed all our lives and to this day I am hugely grateful that he has this basic life skill.

However, while he managed the toilet during the day, he was still wetting the bed at night. This is another very common issue with children, and all too often the parents think their children will simply grow out of it. But it can persist for many years and, in some cases, they do not grow out of it. I have seen plenty of bedwetting nine and ten year olds.

When Brendan was still bedwetting at the age of six, despite our efforts to get him up in the night to use the toilet, we decided to use a 'bell and pad' bedwetting alarm. This kind of alarm, in which the pad detects moisture and sets off the bell, or alarm, has been around for decades. Today's versions are extremely sensitive and safe and are easily available and very effective – the success rate of using them is high but, again, the key is persistence.

The principle is that when the child begins to wet the bed, a bell rings. A plastic pad is placed on the bed under the sheet. It is attached to the alarm by a slim wire which does not disturb the child in bed. The wire is attached to the alarm which sits on the bedside table and goes off as soon as the pad detects moisture.

We found that with Brendan we had to leap up and

grab him to take him to the toilet, the moment the alarm went off. Which meant one of us sleeping nearby next to him for several weeks. And afterwards, if a drop of urine has wet the pad, you have to dry the pad and the sheet before hooking it up again, or the alarm will go off again. We got two sets of pad and alarm, so that after the first incident we replaced the pad with a dry one. It isn't easy; we had to keep at it for weeks, taking turns to be 'on alert' for the bell and to leap up and get Brendan to the toilet. It took several weeks of broken nights. But once he had got it, he began getting up on his own to get to the toilet. And it doesn't always take so long; we re-used the same bell and pad alarm system for Darren a few years later, when he was five, and within two weeks he had stopped bedwetting.

The other aspect of toilet training that is so important is to teach a child to routinely open their bowels with a good diet. Constipation is a huge problem; I see children every day who are suffering from it and figures indicate that as many as one in three children have this problem. Many are being given medication like Movicol, which GPs can prescribe for constipation, but this is not the long term answer and there is almost always no need for it if there is a healthy balanced diet and good toileting habits.

Constipation is usually due to poor eating habits, which all too often lead also to obesity and ill-health. There are rarer causes of constipation due to bowel dysfunction and this needs medical assessment. A child needs a balanced and varied diet, so allowing them to eat only a very limited number of foods can create the problem. Children need plenty of fruit and green vegetables, yoghurts and cereal foods like wholemeal grains. They also need to be taken to the toilet at least once a day – in the morning is best – and encouraged to push out a bowel movement.

All three of our children know that they need to go to the toilet after breakfast. We taught them not to read or distract themselves on the toilet but to concentrate on what they need to do. It is a vital part of being healthy, to keep your bowels working effectively.

I sometimes feel that pets are better disciplined around eating and toilet habits than children. We don't give pets a choice; we give them what is good for them and teach them when and where to go to the toilet. It may seem a little harsh to say we should do the same for children, but they rely on their parents or carers to help them develop healthy habits. They don't know what is good for them until we teach them. As long as parents take charge, invest their time and persist, I believe that many good habits can be achieved.

Quick Tips

- For successful toilet training the key is persistence. If your child learns that you will not be giving up, even the most determined 'toilet-resister' will eventually cooperate. It can take months of perseverance and determination.

- Encourage your child to open their bowels every day by taking them to the toilet at the same time each day – after breakfast is an ideal time. Let them spend some time on the toilet, until going at this time becomes a habit. Use reward charts as positive reinforcement.

- Include plenty of fresh fruit and vegetables as well as yoghurts, grains and cereals in your child's diet, to ensure they have enough roughage.
- Bedwetting is common and can be associated with constipation.
- Consider using an alarm to help resolve bedwetting.

7

Understanding Autism and Its Myths

As I came to terms with Brendan's diagnosis, I wanted to know more about autism, its characteristics and what we, as parents, could do to help him. I felt that I needed to understand the condition and its possibilities and limitations, not only for Brendan's sake, but for my own.

I immersed myself in all the autism books and resources that I could find. Part of acceptance, for me as a paediatrician, was knowledge and awareness. I knew I could not change Brendan's condition, but I knew also that there must be things we could do to help him find ways to cope in a world that would often be daunting and frightening for him.

I had, of course, learned about autism along with a host of other developmental disabilities, during my medical training. But now that my son had been diagnosed, it was intensely personal and I needed to revisit the definition and understand what it may mean for his future.

Autistic Spectrum Disorder (ASD) used to be referred to a group of pervasive developmental disorders (PDD) that includes Autism and Asperger Syndrome. The condition is not immediately obvious but the indicators are usually present from birth and these are characterised by a 'triad of impairments' which were defined in 1979 by the pioneers in the field of childhood development disorders, Lorna Wing and Judith Gould. The triad consists of abnormal functioning in the following areas: 1) Social communication 2) Social interaction and 3) Social imagination and flexibility of thought. In 2013, the American Psychiatric Association updated its diagnostic manual called the Diagnostic and Statistical Manual of Mental Disorders (DSM-5) which describes new guidelines for categorising autism by levels of support. There are three levels, each reflecting a different level of support someone may need. Sometimes signs can be seen in early infancy, while other children will appear to develop normally, and then to suddenly become withdrawn or aggressive or lose language skills they have acquired. Signs are usually seen by two to three years old.

In Brendan's case, I felt certain, looking back, that he displayed traits of ASD from as young as six months old. He would not be interested in our smiles or the funny faces we made and would instead stare at a particular object of his interest for an unusually long time.

The key thing about autism is that there is a spectrum – the condition varies and can manifest through different symptoms. For instance, some children with ASD have difficulty learning, while others have difficulty communicating or adjusting to social situations.

However I never felt comfortable with many of the labels given to those with autism. I felt that to call some people with autism 'low-functioning' and other 'high-functioning' or 'mild' and 'severe' was to pigeonhole children before we had discovered their potential and enabled them to be all they could become.

I recently came across an online joke conversation that very deftly and wittily confronts the way we label and pigeonhole those with autism:

Autistic Person: Are you autistic?

Non-Autistic Person: No.

Autistic Person: What kind of non-autistic are you?

Non-Autistic Person: What do you mean? I never knew that there are different kinds of not being autistic.

Autistic Person: Are you a high-functioning non-autistic or a low-functioning non-autistic?

Non-Autistic Person: What? That doesn't make sense?

Autistic Person: Are you the kind of non-autistic who's independent or do you need other people to help you do certain things? Are you the kind of non-autistic who has amazing skills, or do you struggle with certain things?

Non-Autistic Person: I can't categorise my entire life's experience into one category. There are some things I can do on my own and some things I need help with. There are some things I'm very skilled at, and there are some things that I struggle with.

Autistic Person: Now you know how we feel when people ask us those questions.

This, for me, summed up so much of what is wrong with the way autism is viewed. I was determined never to impose a limit on what Brendan could do and not to make assumptions about his feelings, thoughts or capabilities.

Autism is not directly linked to intelligence. There are those with ASD who are highly intelligent, and others who have low intelligence, just as there are in the community as a whole.

Why does autism occur? We don't yet know. Despite extensive research no specific causes of autism spectrum disorders have yet been found, although many risk factors have been identified in the current research literature that may contribute to the development of these disorders. These include genetics, prenatal and perinatal factors, neuroanatomical abnormalities and environmental factors.

Given the complexity of the disorder, and the fact that symptoms and severity vary, there are probably many causes. Although certain genetic mutations may be a factor there are documented cases of autism occurring in one identical twin but not the other (not dissimilar to cases of Type 1

Diabetes mellitus). Genetics alone, however, can't explain the increasing prevalence of autism.

Meanwhile environmental factors, including everything from viral infections to medications and air pollutants, are the subject of intensive research.

It may, in the end, be a combination of both that lead to autism – a genetic predisposition combined with certain environmental factors. The biggest and most widely circulated controversial debate surrounding the possible cause of autism is the 'vaccine theory'. This theory suggests that autism results from brain damage caused either by (1) the measles, mumps, rubella (MMR) vaccine itself, or by (2) thimerosal, an MMR vaccine stabiliser that contains 50% ethynylmercury. The current scientific and medical consensus worldwide is that no convincing evidence supports these claims.

I was a mother with a recently diagnosed child with autism, and at the same time I was still a trained academic paediatrician. So using all the resources available, I began to fully research the topic. And I am convinced that it was not the MMR vaccine that caused my son to have autism. Darren was almost 12 months old around the time of Brendan's diagnosis and I did not hesitate to give him his MMR vaccination – the benefits of which are indisputable.

Another recent theory about causation of autism arose from the 'elevated foetal testosterone' study suggesting that exposure to high levels of the male hormones testosterone during the foetal stage in the womb contributes to the development of autism. When I was pregnant with Brendan, I had all my routine antenatal screening tests and frequent ultrasound tests which were all reported to be normal. If this theory were to be true, why would my first pregnancy have had exposure to higher testosterone levels than my second or third pregnancies?

People with ASD see, hear and feel the world differently to the rest of us. For many the world can feel overwhelming and make them very anxious. Key among the characteristics is difficulty in interpreting both verbal and non-verbal language, and in 'reading' other people – that is, recognising their signs, meaning, intentions and messages.

Some of those with autism have difficulty with language and other kinds of communication – for instance pictures or sign language – can help. Routines, rules and consistency can be vital to managing in an unpredictable and confusing world. And many with autism have highly-focused interests; an area of interest bordering on the obsessive. Interests may include maths, art, trains, computers, music or perhaps collecting things.

One of the most striking books I read was 'The Reason I Jump' by Naoki Higashida, a 13 year-old boy with non-verbal ASD who learned to write the book using an alphabet grid and who explained, in such clear and simple terms, autism and its associated behaviours.

Reading this book was a revelation. This young Japanese boy opened my eyes to the world of autism – from the inside. He explained in his own words why it was so impossible for him to sit still, what panic attacks were all about and why he spent much of his time stimming – a term which has developed to indicate self-stimulation such as hand-flapping, rocking and spinning. He also explained why he, and others like him, love water so much and how he thinks and feels about nature, other people and himself.

I felt this book opened my eyes to Brendan's world. All Naoki's behaviours were much the same as Brendan's, so for the first time I was able to really see and feel what the behaviours were about. And he confirmed for me that a person with autism has imagination and humour and understands so much, even when they cannot speak.

In the foreword David Mitchell, translator of the book and the parent of a child with autism, talks about how often society makes assumptions about those with autism which are so often wrong. That touched me deeply and reminded me not to assume anything about how Brendan felt or thought.

Naoki pleads with parents not to walk away, however miserable they feel about their child's autism. The child does not know why they are different, and they can't walk away, so we have to stay and be there to help and guide them. I knew, reading his words, that I could never walk away from Brendan. What I wanted was to help him connect with the world and develop his potential as much as possible.

So where, in all of this information, was Brendan? With his significant behavioural issues, restricted interests and social and communicative impairments, it felt daunting to comprehend the challenge ahead and I had no idea where to begin in helping him. For a long time I still felt guilty and afraid that his autism had, in some way, been caused by me. I often felt helpless, and that was a new feeling for me. I didn't talk to Eugene about these feelings because we weren't discussing things much at that time. He wasn't talking about his feelings, or acknowledging the autism much, so I didn't talk about mine. I had to grieve on my own and it felt like a bereavement; grieving for a child I wasn't going to have.

We had to tell our families, and that wasn't easy. We came from a culture that did not acknowledge or accept disability or developmental conditions. My parents were very upset, but they accepted it. My mother had lived with us and cared for Brendan, and she loved him very much. She felt for me, and for us, but she was not with us any longer, to help with the grieving process. Other relatives were in denial for a long time, convinced that there would be a 'cure' and would routinely send us news about 'cures' for autism.

There is no cure, autism is a lifelong condition. We all had to come to terms with this. And over time I began to accept that it was not something I had done, and that if I wanted to give Brendan the best possible chance in life, Eugene and I needed to put aside our sadness, to love Brendan unconditionally and find ways to help him navigate the world around him.

Quick Tips

- In understanding your child's autism, gather as much information as you can, from others in the same situation, from experts, from books, from peer support and from the internet. Be wary that some information online may not be accurate.
- Remember that autism and intellectual disability do not necessarily go hand-in-hand.

- Autism is a spectrum of conditions and each child with autism will have different abilities and learning or behavioural challenges.
- In managing a child with autism, routines and rules can help a great deal. Your child will learn what to expect and what is expected of them.

8

How Can We Help?

The day I accepted that my child had autism was the day I was truly able to start moving on. That came at least a year after Brendan's diagnosis. But in the meantime I managed my disbelief and grief by learning everything I could about current therapies for autism.

Over a period of months I enrolled myself, and Eugene, in a number of courses and programmes intended to help improve our communication with Brendan. We knew not everything would work, it was going to be a question of trial and error. But we felt sure that *some* things would work; we just had to find out what.

Our courses included:

It Takes Two to Talk by The Hanen Centre
More than Words by The Hanen Centre

Early Bird Programme
Early Bird Plus Programme
British Signalong
Makaton Language Programme
TEACCH Approach
Applied Behavioural Analysis and private speech therapist

For contact details for all these courses see the information section at the back of the book.

Two of these early courses were run by The Hanen Centre, a charity based in Ontario, Canada, but with a global reach, including a number of speech therapists running workshops in the UK. The Hanen Centre aims to address delays in language development in young children, including those with autism, and to enable these children to develop the best possible language skills. The workshops are for parents and professionals working with young children.

These courses were, at the time of writing, still available and of great value, but of course there are now constant fresh developments in autism research, understanding and help, so do check locally to see what there is that might benefit you and your child (and see the information section at the end of this book).

When we started going to Hanen Centre workshops, I still believed that Brendan's problems might be largely about speech and language. In the event this was only a part of his condition, but what we learned through the Hanen teaching was extremely useful. Communication with others is such a vital part of being human; it allows us to connect with others, to have relationships, to let people know how we feel and to make our wants known.

I was drawn to The Hanen Centre's ethos and methods. They say 'Research has continually shown that early intervention can make a huge difference in improving the communication skills of children on the autism spectrum. In particular, the research shows that when parents interact with their children in ways that motivate, encourage and support their child's communication, they can make a significant difference to their child's social and communication development.' (The Hanen Centre, www. hanen.org).

The Hanen Centre aims to show parents and teachers how to do this.

It Takes Two to Talk

This course was targeted at parents of children with speech and language delays rather than specifically for those with Autistic Spectrum Disorder. I went along on this course anyway and picked up useful tips that I still use today.

The course is based on research that shows that children learn language best when they are allowed to lead a conversation and communicate about what interests them. When parents apply what is known as the 'Observe-Wait-Learn' (OWL) strategy, parents can get in tune with their child's interests and communication style and then follow the child's lead(The Hanen Centre, www.hanen.org). The longer children stay in these responsive interactions with their parents, the more practice, feedback and language they will learn, all of which builds their communication skills.

In Brendan's case, I had to modify it slightly as it was unlikely that Brendan would ever initiate or lead a conversation. What I did do was join in with Brendan's interest in cars and trains. I started playing alongside him saying, 'vroom vroom' and mimicking his fascination with wheels for long minutes until momentarily he would glance over at what I was doing and sometimes mimic a 'vroom'. This felt like an achievement, a small step forward on the path to communicating with my son.

More Than Words

This was a course aimed at the parents of children with Autistic Spectrum Disorder and other social communication difficulties. Eugene and I attended in the evenings on a weekly basis for three months.

The course helped parents to become their child's primary language facilitator and to understand and accommodate their child's sensory preferences. It enabled us to provide the structure and predictability that would help our child to learn, as well as integrating the strategies that support the child's social interaction and communication into their everyday activities and routines.

It was on this course that I learned about Brendan's sensory processing disorders (SPD) and began to understand that loud noises or certain types of clothing could agitate him. I realised that his constant need to jump about all the time was not because he was being naughty or misbehaving but was actually a coping mechanism to dampen down the difficulties he encountered with the SPD.

Eugene and I learned to play rough and tumble games with Brendan, using his need for vigorous movement to encourage his communication with us. There were interactive group training sessions and individual videotaping feedback sessions where we could analyse with the therapist what went well and what could be done better to maximise and retain the strategies we had learned, in order to improve our communication with Brendan.

It also taught us an approach called 'Owling' or Observe, Wait and Listen. This involved watching Brendan closely, observing his facial expressions and actions, to see what he was interested in. For example we bought him a Playmobil farm set. We soon realised that he wasn't interested in the little people or animals, but in the tractor, and, specifically, its wheels. I would sit quietly just watching him play, waiting and listening for any messages he would send me, verbally or physically, about what he liked or didn't like and what he wanted to do. I learned to really see Brendan, and to understand what he enjoyed.

It took time and patience, and I am not always the most patient of people, but it was so worthwhile. By Owling, I learned that although Brendan was non-verbal, he was indeed trying to communicate with me, and I created a list of sounds he made which, over time, I came to understand as his substitute for language.

In this way, I was able to construct Brendan's baseline speech which I later shared with his nursery special needs teachers and his speech and language therapists and using Nuffield Intensive speech therapy, we began building his speech.

Example of Brendan's baseline speech is shown below

Word	Brendan's speech (consistently)
Mummy	Ma Ma
Papa	Pa
No	Ga
Yes	Ya
Milk	Ba
car	Arr
Monsters Inc	Ba ee
dirty	Ee
Wee wee	Wa wa
water	Wa peh or wa
Kung Fu Panda	'A' 'oo' 'p'
Swimming	Wa pi
Park	pa
Playground	pa
Wall-E	Wa ee
Poo poo	Pee (usually points to bum)
McDonald's	Mm ba
Dog	ga
pringle	pee
pain	Pee (action pointing to area that is painful)
play	pee

big	Bah ga (also uses hand sign for big)
small	Ahh (uses hand sign for small)
Tesco	Eh oh
Corn flakes	Ah fff
boots	bah
pig	'P' 'ig'
one	ah
two	ee
Pinky ponk	Pee ah
open	Ah pi

The Early Bird course is one that I would highly recommend for parents of newly diagnosed young children with Autistic Spectrum Disorder. It really made a difference to us, both in our understanding of what was happening for Brendan and in our ability to find ways of getting through to him.

Early Bird Programme

This programme, run by the National Autistic Society (NAS), was developed to support parents and carers during the period between early diagnosis (under 4 years of age) and school placement in the UK. It aimed to bridge the gap in educational provision for pre-school aged children with ASD.

The NAS says, 'It will help you understand your child's autism; get yourself into your child's world, make contact, and find ways to develop interaction and communication; and learn how to analyse and understand your child's behaviours and how to use structure, so you can pre-empt and cope with problem behaviours'. (The National Autistic Society, www.autism.or.uk).

Eugene and I attended this course on a weekly basis for three months and it helped us in developing useful techniques at home, both for helping and encouraging Brendan's social communication and for pre-empting the development of inappropriate behaviours.

Rewards were the way to improve his good behaviours and we used a lot of star charts to show Brendan visually what progress he was making and to encourage him to earn a reward if he continued to earn the stars.

As far as possible we worked on encouraging the behaviours we wanted, while ignoring those we didn't, such as meltdowns. Of course we didn't always manage this – it can be very difficult if your child is screaming and throwing themselves about, but it's better, as far as possible, to avoid doing anything that might prolong or intensify your child's upset and distress. Quietly and calmly ignoring it is the most effective way to allow your child to calm down and let the anxieties dissipate.

Consistency in the family and between you and your partner is really crucial. So agree in advance what each of you will do if your child is upset and unable to control themselves.

The therapist would make home visits to observe our play and interaction with Brendan, using communication techniques taught in the course. I also found it useful to be able to talk to other parents who were in a similar situation with a child recently diagnosed with ASD.

Early Bird Plus Programme

This is a similar programme to the initial Early Bird course but is tailored towards the parents and carers of children diagnosed later, between 4 to 8 years old, who have already started school. The programme is structured with weekly attendance by a parent and a school representative who will both work with the child regularly at school over the three months. The course focuses on both the home and school environment and aims to work to build a close relationship between the parent and the school representative in achieving targets to develop social skills and communication.

I attended this programme Early Bird Plus when Brendan was at school with one of his teaching assistants and I found it very helpful in gaining a close working relationship with her. This particular programme was useful in that it was aimed at bringing together the therapies at home and in school so that there was consistency. It also gave me confidence, knowing that whatever we were doing at home that worked well with Brendan was being duplicated at school and vice versa.

British Signalong

The primary purpose of Signalong was to assist with communication in cases of language problems associated with learning disabilities. Signalong is based on British Sign Language and most of the signs are unaltered, but there are a few which have been adapted for ease of use with an ASD child.

When Brendan was still unable to communicate a single word at the age of three, he often became increasingly frustrated at his inability to tell us what he wanted. He couldn't point, either, so he really had no way of letting us know if he wanted a certain toy, or food, or anything else. It was frustrating for us too, seeing his distress.

We had a speech therapist at the time who taught us to use British Signalong as a way of communicating with Brendan. Eugene and I went on the British Signalong course and earned a beginner's certificate.

This was a valuable non-verbal method of communicating with Brendan and it helped us understand and reinforce communication by signing to Brendan at the same time.

Because Brendan was a non-verbal in the early years, we would become frustrated, and so would he, when he was trying to communicate something to us that we couldn't understand. This often led to many meltdowns.

Using British Signalong and Makaton, we could teach him hand gestures to say 'eat' 'drink' 'more' 'please' and so on. We would use these gestures and he learned to mimic us when he wanted something specific.

Over the following years Brendan continued to sign as he was learning to speak. One of the BBC television programmes that was very helpful in encouraging the use of Signalong was Mr Tumble which was, luckily, also one of Brendan's favourite programmes. Mr Tumble uses a lot of Makaton and similar concepts, with a simple repetitive format, making it easy to learn the Makaton symbols and signs used in each episode. Children are encouraged to join in with activities, songs and games and Brendan loved Mr Tumble and its games and songs.

Makaton Language Programme

The Makaton Language Programme is also widely used in the UK.

Makaton is a language programme using signs and symbols alongside speech to help people to communicate. It is designed to support spoken language and the signs and symbols are used in spoken word order. The idea is that as speech develops the signs and symbols can be dropped naturally, at the child's own pace.

In Makaton you use the British Signalong and graphic signs and symbols together. It was helpful to learn about Makaton which we were taught simultaneously when we were learning to use the British Signalong, although Eugene and I did not choose to use the entire Makaton programme for Brendan at the time, we did not feel it necessary since many of its concepts were similar to the strategies we were already using to enable better communication with Brendan.

TEACCH Approach

Many schools within the UK have adopted the TEACCH approach (Treatment and Education of Autistic and related

Communication Handicapped Children) in educating children with ASD. This method involves individualised programmes of activities based on the developmental profile of each child. One of our speech therapists was extremely well-trained in autism intervention methods and she introduced us to this programme, to be undertaken both at school and at home. In Brendan's case, it involved a series of tasks which he was required to complete in order to gain a reward. Some tasks would be catered towards his ability to achieve that task, for example matching the pictures to the objects. Some tasks were used to stretch his ability to improve his fine motor coordination, for example threading beads and completing a puzzle. We would get Brendan to do multiple different tasks for short periods of time several times a day, both at school and at home.

Brendan was not at all cooperative at first, so we came up with immediate short-term rewards such as having one of his favourite Pringle crisps after he had completed the smallest task and then expanding the task, while at the same time reducing the number and frequency of the Pringles.

It took a lot of perseverance, and both Eugene and I had to be committed to complete the series of tasks with Brendan every day. It could take more than an hour for the simplest of tasks at first, but it did get better with time and it really was worthwhile, so I would urge anyone to persevere and not give up.

Applied Behavioural Analysis

Applied Behavioural Analysis (ABA) or behavioural modification is a different psychological approach which relies on external reinforcement and behavioural learning theory as the primary means to engage children in tasks to modify their behaviour and to teach them the basic skills they need to know.

Unlike TEACCH, ABA is not concerned with unobservable variables such as how the child thinks and integrates information; the focus is solely on observable behaviours and teaching the child to interact with normally functioning peers. ABA teaches the child eye contact, play skills, receptive language and behaviour, expressive language, colours, categories, numbers and so on. In the same way that we train animals, ABA motivates children with rewards such as praise or food and it ignores the 'unwanted behaviours'. It is an all-encompassing programme involving the entire family and it can take up to 40 hours per week as each part of the child's activity or schedule is overseen by the ABA therapist or parent. It is expensive and it is not offered by the NHS in the UK.

We initially employed a private ABA therapist to train us and work with Brendan at home in the early years to observe his behaviours. Using positive reinforcement and prompting, we would learn to reward Brendan with star charts and Pringle crisps for any desirable or positive behaviour that he displayed, such as asking for something during a play session or using his visual cards when he wanted an item or toy, while at the same time reducing his negative and undesirable behaviours by removing any triggers.

There were many of these negative behaviours – Brendan would, for instance, shout, drop to the floor screaming, throw his plate of food or drink and refuse to shower or to clean his teeth. But for each successful behaviour he was rewarded with a star on the chart that would eventually allow him to earn a toy that he really wanted.

Quick Tips

- To find out exactly what courses are available in your area, get in touch with your local council's special educational needs department and speech and language department.
- Devise visual reward systems to use with your child. Use stars and charts to show them their progress and to offer rewards for tasks completed.
- As far as possible, ignore difficult behaviours and concentrate on encouraging the positive and cooperative behaviours.
- Challenging behaviours, distress and anxiety can stem from your child's frustration at not being able to communicate.
- Be consistent in your approach between carers when implementing a behavioural intervention.
- Many children require an individualised approach and it is up to us to find out what works and what does not work for them.

9

The Power of Pictures

By the time Brendan was four, he still showed no signs of speaking any meaningful words. The developmental progress of a three to four year old should include well over 500 words and he or she should be able to describe things and situations in a meaningful way. Brendan could only say 'mama' and 'papa' for his mum and dad, and would substitute sounds such as 'ga' for no and 'ya' for yes. The delay in speech and communication skills were hallmarks of ASD but I could not help but wonder if Brendan's speech problems were purely related to the ASD diagnosis, or if there was something else I was missing.

I was faced with a daily dose of extreme frustration from a child who was not able to communicate his wants and needs. My frustrations were on par with his when I was not able to guess what it was that he was trying to say. The exchanges would frequently end up with one or both of us in tears.

By this time we had begun on the round of courses, aimed at helping to improve our communication with Brendan. But we still had a long way to go, there was no sudden breakthrough and I searched constantly for a way to help him.

I decided to try using the system of Picture Exchange Communication System (PECS), which I had come across during my research into autism. PECS uses visual pictures and symbols as a form of communication; at its most basic, the child hands you, or indicates, a picture of what they want. It encouraged Brendan to engage with me and initiate a communication.

One of Brendan's favourite snacks was Pringles crisps, so we started by teaching him to exchange the picture of a Pringle with a real Pringle. We would put the picture of the Pringle beside him and the packet of Pringles nearby. He had to pick up the picture of the Pringle and hand it to us, and we would then hand him a real Pringle. He got the hang of it very quickly, which was exciting for us.

We slowly extended the range, using pictures of his favourite toys which we kept out of his reach until he 'asked' for them with a picture. Within days, Brendan was able to request his trucks and Lego by giving us pictures of them.

PECS is extended over several stages over a period of time. Brendan soon learned to use two symbols; the first for 'I want' and the second for whatever the item was. PECS also taught him to be able to point. He had never done this before, but now he could point to a PECS picture that we had stuck on a wall or door and tell us what he wanted. He became so good at communicating his wants and needs that I soon realised that, for a child who never uttered a word, he had a very large vocabulary and did understand a lot more than I gave him credit for.

All the PECS cards had to be made by us – we would take a photo of the item or place, and then make a laminated card that we could put up, or use for Brendan to exchange. I ended up spending hours each day taking pictures of everything, from a range of possible food choices to all his toys, and making them into PECS cards. We ended up with dozens of cards, stuck all over the house. But it was worth all the effort involved, we had found another way for Brendan to communicate with us.

We were delighted, but I was also aware that not everyone thought PECS was a good idea. Some health professionals at the time felt that the use of a non-verbal communication system might make it less likely that Brendan would ever learn how to speak. This concerned me, so I researched it and found that there is no evidence to indicate that visual aids, visual cues or the use of PECS cards would interfere or inhibit the development of speech in later years.

In fact there is a growing belief in the speech therapists community that systems such as PECS have a beneficial impact on speech development and reduce the frustration and anxiety caused to children by their lack of speech. Brendan was a testament to this. He became an effective communicator and there were far fewer tears in our household once PECS was in place and part of our everyday life.

I began to fill folders with PECS cards, so that Brendan could leaf through and find the thing he wanted. I made cards for a whole range of colours and numbers as well as words such as big and little. In this way Brendan began learning to put sequences of cards together, combining three or four words to construct simple sentences. Soon he was putting together three and four word sentences and before long these grew. At one time his favourite was, 'I want-big-yellow-train-and-2-Pringles'. I was impressed by his ability to pick these words and put them together. He knew exactly what he wanted to say, he just hadn't had the words before.

As he steadily progressed in his PECS communication, I began making PECS step-by-step sequences for each routine that Brendan was required to learn. There was one for how to brush his teeth, another for showering, drying himself and getting dressed, and another for using the toilet, flushing and washing his hands. These timetables were stuck all around the house and the minor embarrassment when visitors came was more than worth the progress that Brendan made. Following the sequences helped him towards a degree of independence that had, not long before, seemed impossible.

PECS made an enormous difference to Brendan. But while the system was cheap and simple, I was still spending hours each day making and updating the laminated cards, often doing this late into the night. I knew we couldn't continue with this system forever, it was a big step forward, but I was aware that we needed to move on to something more advanced – not least because carrying big folders of PECS cards around was impractical – I couldn't take them out with us when we went shopping or on outings and even carrying them around the house was becoming difficult.

PECS and other communication aids are low-tech in that they don't involve an external power source. But there are other, more sophisticated aids which supplement or replace speech, known in the speech therapy world as Augmentative and Alternative Communication (AAC). These require an external power source such as batteries or electricity. I began looking into these, to see if there was something that might work for Brendan.

AAC aids permit the storage and retrieval of electronic messages and allow the user to communicate using a speech output. For example, when the symbol is touched on the device, it produces a voice saying the word out loud at the same time.

I sought help from my local speech therapists and from the Advisory Centre for Education (ACE) in Manchester which provides free advice to parents on all aspects of state-funded education for special needs children. After multiple enquiries and letters both within the UK and in the USA, I eventually managed to get educational funding for a device called the Vantage Lite, or 'Liberator' – an electronic voice output device with simple keyboard options. It looked like a chunky version of a today's iPad and we were able to download hundreds of PECS symbols, words and numbers onto it.

The Liberator was well suited to Brendan's age, development and size as it was portable, lightweight, easy to use and it could be programmed to progress as Brendan's communication improved. Brendan loved it from the moment he worked out how to use it and we loved it the moment we realised we could get rid of the volumes of folders filled with laminated PECS symbols. Brendan's Vantage Lite communication aid became his 'voice'. He would simply type or press the symbol, word or number and a sentence would be formed. He could then touch the 'speak' button and a 'voice' sounding very like a human boy would say the words, giving Brendan a voice. He began to take it everywhere with him and it meant that, in one aspect at least, life was a little simpler. The teaching staff at school could understand Brendan when he was using the Liberator device to 'speak' to them and they learned to use the Liberator to communicate with him. More than a decade later, there are now symbol-supported communication apps like Proloquo2Go which can be programmed directly into an Android or iPad.

While I continued to look for every means possible to help Brendan, we had increasing concerns about Darren. He was now two and, as with Brendan, his speech was also delayed.

We hardly dared to think it – but could our second son also have ASD? Certainly he was not speaking, and this had been the primary sign that alerted me to a problem with Brendan. But in other respects Darren was a very different child. He had always been easy in almost every respect. He ate, slept and behaved, for the most part, without problems. If anything I felt guilty for giving him less attention because I had so much time and energy focussed on Brendan.

Worryingly Darren began to imitate some of Brendan's troubled behaviour – in particular his meltdowns; shouting, screaming and rolling on the floor. I became increasingly concerned. Darren had a hearing test, but passed it – we were told that hearing was not the problem. Our hearts sank – why wasn't he speaking? What could it be? I hoped not autism, and it didn't seem so, because Darren also sought affection and attention, which Brendan never did.

At this time we had a wonderful Polish au pair, Theresa. Unlike most au pairs she was older; in her early fifties. She was Polish and her English was very broken as this was her first trip outside Poland. She had brought up her own children and she wanted to experience something different in life. For us she was a godsend; sensible, experienced and capable. She was with us for two years, and we wished it could have been longer.

Theresa took Brendan to nursery from the age of three. He went without a fuss, but he stayed separate from the group, refusing to join in any activities. He was always preoccupied and in his own little world. He didn't like to be touched or cuddled and he didn't interact with any children or adults.

Once Darren was two, Theresa took him to nursery with Brendan, but although he didn't speak, Darren's behaviour was very different – he smiled and clapped and liked to play with the other children or to have a hug from the nursery teachers. So we were hopeful that Darren did not have autism.

Jane, the speech therapist who had helped us with Brendan, came to see Darren when he was two and a half. She had him formally tested for autism and the result was negative. But he did have a severe speech delay.

We worked with Darren with the PECS system and with British Signalong too, and it was a great help. I had stopped speaking Chinese to Brendan when the speech therapist said it was simpler for him to learn only one language, and I stopped with Darren too, hoping it would help. But he didn't start to speak and we continued to be puzzled by what could be wrong.

It was not until almost two years later, when Darren was four, that he was routinely given a hearing test as part of the school's screening programme. After three failed hearing tests we discovered the problem was, after all, loss of hearing. He had moderate to severe sensorineural hearing loss on both sides. It seemed that his pass for the earlier hearing tests had been an error due to equipment failure in the hospital.

It was heart breaking to think that he couldn't speak because he simply couldn't hear. But in finding the diagnosis, we also found the solution. Darren was given hearing aids and they changed his world. He found every sound amazing. The sound of the running washing machine, the television, an aeroplane – everything amazed him and with each new sound he would turn to us, eyes wide. and say, 'What's that?'

Of course we wondered why he had the hearing problem. Through a genetics assessment, it seems that Eugene and I both carried the Connexion 26 gene mutation which is one of the most common causes of congenital sensorineural hearing loss. The child needs to inherit the recessive gene from both parents for the hearing loss to be active. Carriers with the gene have a one in two chance of passing it to their children who would be a carrier of the gene but not be affected unless they inherited both genetic defects from both parents. We'd had no idea, and while we felt saddened by this, and by the delay in diagnosis, we were delighted with Darren's progress once the problem was spotted.

It took him a while to get used to the hearing aids, but bit by bit he did. And it took him two years to catch up in his speech. Before we discovered the problem he had been rated with a severe speech deficiency of 0.1% function, which meant he would be unable to enter a mainstream school. He was put into a speech and language special school where he was in a class of only six and the teachers used PECS and British Signalong. But once he could hear, and learn to speak, within two years Darren went back into the mainstream system and was found to be exceptionally bright. Since then Darren has flourished, doing well in his academic work, becoming school captain and joining the school council as well as playing the piano, saxophone and enjoying strong friendships with other children.

For Darren, the way forward appeared brighter. But for Brendan, there was still so much to learn, to understand and to do in order to make his world as safe and happy as possible.

Quick Tips

- If you are concerned about your child's hearing ask your doctor for a test, and for a second opinion, if necessary.
- With a special needs child you need to be ready to research and investigate all possible sources of help and support.

- Picture card systems like PECS and AAC devices can make a dramatic difference with children with special needs including autism, speech impairment and deafness.

10

Searching for Answers

It was not easy to pour out my frustrations on others at work; neither did I feel I could vent my worries and concerns to my husband, who already had so much on his plate. So I turned to social media, and it gave me a way to feel that I wasn't alone.

At first I simply researched, but later I participated in autism forums and discussions on chat forums, websites and Facebook. Being able to participate anonymously gave me a sense of personal security and I soon learned just how many parents and families felt unheard and unsupported by society and healthcare professionals. It was a huge problem.

Many parents talked about feeling abandoned once the diagnosis of autism was made for their child. Shocked and distressed, they were simply left to cope on their own, as best they could, with this life-altering diagnosis. Many parents have told me that no support, or even information, was provided once the diagnosis was made. So these parents went away, while still coming to terms with the situation and wondering what on earth the future would be like for them and for their child, and tried on their own to research any possible avenues of help.

To add to this, many local authorities, under pressure of budget cuts, have reduced specialist support and parental courses. So even when parents can find out, on their own, what is available, it often isn't much. So much more needs to be done.

The late diagnosis of autism was another much-discussed subject. All too often the diagnosis had been made when the child was starting school at five or even older. Yet, early diagnosis of the autistic spectrum can lead to early intervention and access to special education programmes which can make a real difference.

In clinics I often saw parents who told me their child with autism never slept, or took off all their clothes in public, self harmed or screamed constantly. These obsessive behaviours can easily drive any exhausted parent to the brink. In the internet chats a lot of parents said that when dealing with medical staff in hospitals and clinics, they felt insignificant and unimportant, as medical staff discussed their child in front of them, without including them and then made recommendations without offering any further support. A lot of these discussions were about things that I had either witnessed or had been through too, so I was able to share their experiences. And as a paediatrician it was helpful for me to hear what parents wanted from medical staff; to be consulted, included and listened to and to be given an idea of where to find support and information. None of these things seems too much to ask.

As parents of a child with autism, in the anonymous cloud of the internet, we gave each other support as we were all going through the same challenges, fears and emotions. Being able to talk, to express our fears and frustrations and to swap information and experiences was a huge help.

While the internet gave me, and others, a lot of support, the danger is that more and more 'therapies' can be found online as alternative treatments for ASD. And many of these therapies are not clinically tested or scientifically proven and are not only expensive, but potentially harmful. The internet today is a minefield of miracle cures. Some sources say autism is a form of allergy that can be cured by a change of diet; others say it is a vitamin deficiency. Another says it is a fungal infection that can be cured with antifungal therapy and no doubt more 'experts' will come up with yet more cures as time goes on. Each claimed treatment always seems to produce parents who will swear it has cured their child of autism. But either their children did not have autism or they are not being truthful.

Reading about supposedly 'miraculous' treatments I felt very strongly the twin pull of being a mother and a doctor. As a mother, I was always searching for answers or possible cures. I would forget about being a doctor and succumb to wild tales of cures as a result of these alternative treatments, a surge of hope allowing me to imagine, for a moment, Brendan without autism. I was so tempted. But as a doctor with over two decades of experience in scientific research,

I knew that I had to be extremely careful before trying any possible unproven treatment.

Initially I ruled out invasive and possibly harmful treatments, but decided I would consider others that would not cause harm. And some of them did seem worth testing. So we tried Brendan on B12 and omega fatty acids supplements, but we found that they made no difference after six months. We also considered acupuncture, but when we contemplated holding a screaming child down as the acupuncturist tried to put the needles into him, it was a definite no.

I do empathise with all the parents out there who hold onto a glimmer of hope that someday someone will find a cure. In the light of so many claims online that such and such a therapy has cured someone's child how hard it is not to hope. I know that I am that parent on some days. But the price for trying out untested and invasive treatments can be high.

I know of a woman who, against all medical advice, took her child to Germany to undergo three days of plasmapheresis treatment. This is a process, not unlike kidney dialysis, in which a machine is used to remove the blood, treat or replace the plasma, and return it to the patient. It is an invasive and risky procedure that could endanger a child's life. Thankfully this child was alright, although the side-effects of nausea and dizziness would have been extremely unpleasant. The treatment did not cure her son of autism, and it ended up costing her a small fortune.

Many people would condemn this mother, but she did it not because she was a bad mother but because she was afraid that if she didn't pursue that course of treatment she would have missed out on a cure. I cannot criticise parents who opt for alternative non-medically proven methods of therapy, hoping against hope that something will help their child's condition. On the other hand, I cannot condone the reckless false advertisements of companies claiming that their methods have 'cured' children, simply in order to make money. Such claims are hugely irresponsible.

As a paediatrician, I would warn parents against using the internet to obtain information on possible miracle cures for ASD. Over the years, more and more therapies can be found online, all claiming that they will cure autism. These include plasmapheresis, stem cell treatment, antifungal medications, acupuncture, hyperbaric oxygen treatment and nutritional therapies with vitamin B12, magnesium and omega fatty acids. There are countless published anecdotes on the web for each of these alternative methods that state that it has benefited children with ASD. However, there has been no conclusive research designed to evaluate any of these interventions or to measure treatment effectiveness in improving ASD symptoms. Many of these therapies are not only expensive, but they could be harmful. They offer parents false hope – far better to go to autism experts to find out what will be most effective in helping children and their families to manage ASD.

There is no scientific evidence that elimination of casein, dairy or gluten in the diet improves the symptoms of ASD in children, but some parents, doctors and researchers say that children with autism have shown mild to dramatic improvements in speech and or behaviour after gluten (found in wheat, barley, rye and oats) and dairy were removed from their diets.

While as a paediatrician, I couldn't find any scientific evidence or consensus among scientists on advocating a 'Gluten-Free and Casein-Free' diet as a treatment for autism, as a mother I would have done anything to help Brendan and I knew that trying a diet for a while would not hurt him. Since there was a good amount of anecdotal evidence around, Eugene and I decided to give it a try to see if it had any effect on Brendan's speech and behaviour.

I started out by eliminating all gluten from his diet which was a feat in itself as Brendan adored McDonald's meals, cornflakes and nuggets. No more flour, wheat or any other tasty ingredients for the family, as what Brendan ate we all had to eat as well. It would have been too unkind if we had eaten forbidden foods in front of him.

That diet was a time when I really empathised with my patients who had coeliac disease, necessitating a lifelong gluten-free diet. Back then, only a tiny section of any supermarket was allocated to products that are gluten-free and the choices were limited and uninspiring. Privately Eugene and I agreed that most of the gluten-free food we tried tasted like cardboard. Thankfully there are far better and tastier gluten-free food options today.

We persevered for six whole months, forcing Brendan to eat substitute gluten-free bread and fake cornflakes, both of which he loathed. I kept a diary of symptoms during those six months and found no difference in his behaviour or abilities.

We then eliminated all dairy products (containing the potential allergen casein) from his diet as well as maintaining the gluten-free diet. This was doubly difficult. We replaced Brendan's favourite cow's milk with soya milk and all his dairy yoghurts with soya ones. He hated them and would shout, spit and throw the food to the ground, unable to understand why we'd taken away the foods he loved. It took a toll on the entire family – it was hard to create meals without these foods and none of us enjoyed the substitutes – and I must admit that I would sometimes sneak a piece of bread when Brendan was not around.

At the six month mark, Eugene and I found there had been no significant changes or improvements. We conceded defeat and agreed to resume Brendan's normal diet.

Why had some people reported an improvement in their child on these diets? I think it was probably that their children had gastrointestinal problems or food intolerances, so the diet would have calmed their intestinal tract and helped regulate their bowels, and this might have led to calmer behaviour, meaning that some improvement due to the dietary change is still plausible.

In the long term I would also worry about the impact of eliminating all dairy products in a diet which may cause bone-thinning and decrease bone development in children due to calcium and vitamin D deficiency.

I was incredibly disappointed that the diet hadn't made any difference, but when I saw Brendan happily eat his McDonald's nuggets again, I realised that it may have been a blessing in disguise – Brendan can simply go ahead and enjoy the foods he likes. He's always been a fussy eater, rejecting some foods, eating his meals in a particular order, one food at a time and keeping everything very clearly separate on his plate, but none of these habits does any harm and the foods he enjoys give him real pleasure.

Another treatment I came across was Neurofeedback, also known as Neurotherapy or Neurobiofeedback. This is a treatment that uses real-time displays of brain activity, obtained through sensors placed on the skull, to teach the subject to control behaviour. It is often used for hyperactivity, or Attention-Deficit-Hyperactivity-Disorder (ADHD). The feedback from the sensors will help identify what activity is giving rise to certain symptoms. The idea is to train parts of the brain, just as exercise trains our muscles.

Brendan was diagnosed with ADHD when he was seven and it had caused us a lot of concern as he was extremely hyperactive, aggressive and was unable to concentrate at school. He was also completely unaware of dangers and in particular the fear that he would hurt himself when he was throwing himself around during a meltdown.

We had already tried Ritalin, the most widely-used drug treatment, without success, and then other forms of ADHD drugs, Equasym and Concerta, also without success. When Brendan was eight we saw a private neuropsychiatrist who suggested we try the Neurofeedback. This was not funded by the NHS and we had to privately pay for the assessment and sessions.

During the sessions, when the individual produces the correct brainwave, they are rewarded by a visual movement or auditory sound, therefore reinforcing the behaviour. In other words, you are playing a game or watching a video by using your brainwaves instead of your hands. As the patient has more training sessions, the brain has to work harder to get rewarded. On average, an individual would expect to have 40 sessions of Neurofeedback treatment with each session approximately one hour long and occurring at least once a week.

An electroencephalogram (EEG) which is a measure of brain activity is done at the outset and then when the neurofeedback sessions have been completed, another EEG is recorded. This can be compared to the original one and will show the progress that has been made during the training sessions.

There was no pain involved and Brendan didn't mind the sensors being placed on his head, once he was distracted with a favourite toy. So we went through three months of these sessions and as the training sessions went on, Brendan became much calmer and was able to sit still for much longer periods of time. However this could have been purely coincidental, because he enjoyed concentrating on the game which was very much like the Pac-man game he loved, simply using the brain to control the movements rather than his hands.

I was never entirely sure how successful this neurofeedback therapy was overall, and since it was very costly and had to be privately funded I would be cautious in recommending it to anyone else.

We stopped after three months, as the improvements in terms of Brendan's concentration and screaming fits began to plateau so we felt there was unlikely to be any further significant benefit.

I still find the internet a valuable source of forums and discussion sites. I have picked up useful tips, shared experiences and made friends. One of these was another mother, Christine, who wrote a blog about her son. He was a little older than Brendan but going through very similar issues with behaviour and speech. She had been through many of the same courses and her warm, articulate account of all that she and her family went through was comforting and inspiring. Christine was – and is – an amazing woman, a fighter who stands up for her son and who loves him dearly.

Quick Tips

- Social media can be used as a platform to connect with others, to share information and to engage in informal peer support.
- The internet can be a valuable resource for gathering information about all aspects of coping with autism but do please be careful about unproven therapies.
- Before you try any new strategy on your child, be certain that it can do no harm.
- Accept that there are no miracle 'cures' but there are plenty of ways to help your child.

11

Starting School

As Brendan approached school age, I was determined that he would go to a mainstream school.

Why? I think I was still in denial and was yet to face the full extent of his autism. I felt that since Brendan, like all children with ASD, would have to manage in a world designed for non-autistic people that it might be better for him to start off in a regular environment and that he could learn and adapt to school and would have better role models being with regular, non-autistic (neurotypical) children in a mainstream school.

This was perhaps more wishful thinking on my part than anything else, since the evidence is clear that children with autism on the whole do better in a specialist environment. But I was also certain at the time that his speech difficulties were his primary problem and that these could be resolved in time. Tests had shown that he was of normal intelligence, so I believed it was just a question of finding the best way to teach him.

One thing is certain; after a diagnosis of autism, you are faced with a schooling minefield.

Firstly, before a school can be determined, a child with a diagnosis of any learning-related condition must have what used to be called a statement of special educational needs, which is now known as an Education, Health and Care Plan (EHCP). This can take quite some time, so from the age of three until he was five Brendan was put into a specialised assessment unit for children awaiting educational statements. He had therapies there whilst he was waiting for a place in a special needs school.

In the United Kingdom, a child by the age of 5 must receive suitable full-time education. This requires parents to decide on which school to choose and registering their child at the school. If a child is pre-school age (under 5) and is undergoing a statutory assessment of his/her educational needs, for reasons such as an ASD diagnosis, your local authority should provide you with a list of suitable schools that are close to you. They may provide you with a complete list of mainstream and specialist providers with guidance on which may be the right places to look at, or they may give you a select list of schools that they feel are right for your child. You can ask for a more comprehensive list if you feel you do not have enough information and I would recommend visiting the schools before making any decisions. The statement of special educational needs or EHCP is necessary in order to access a place at a special school.

In Brendan's case the authorities at the specialist assessment unit wanted to put him into a special needs school for those with severe learning difficulties, but I disagreed. He had been diagnosed with verbal dyspraxia and was non-verbal. They appeared to have made the assumption that Brendan's cognitive abilities and intelligence were low because he was non-verbal. I knew that Brendan was a lot more able than he appeared and I believed that helping Brendan learn to speak was the most important thing to concentrate on and that it could be helped in a mainstream school with intensive speech therapy.

Dyspraxia means difficulty with learned patterns of movement in the absence of damage to the muscles or the nerves. A child with physical dyspraxia will usually have generalised motor difficulties – where the child has problems co-ordination of gross and fine body movements. (These children were once called 'clumsy children'.)

A child who has been diagnosed as dyspraxic by a speech and language therapist will have developmental verbal dyspraxia (sometimes referred to as developmental articulatory dyspraxia). This is characterised by marked difficulties in producing speech sounds and in sequencing them together into words. In addition, such children will often have difficulty in making and coordinating the precise movements of the lips, tongue and palate required to produce speech. This was the case with Brendan. A huge part of Brendan's frustrations came from his inability to communicate with us. And it was an inability to speak, rather than a refusal to speak.

I was told that Brendan's autism required a special school,

but I was in denial and grief for a long time. I didn't accept what I was being told; that the autism needed just as much attention, if not more attention, than verbal dyspraxia. I still believed his autism was moderate and could be managed in a mainstream school and no-one dared to tell me that it was much more severe than I thought.

Every child awaiting placement in a special educational needs school should have an assessment by an educational psychologist to determine their level of cognition and intelligence. The schools vary widely, so the child could be placed in a special school that was for children with severe learning difficulties or one for children with mild to moderate learning difficulties.

My appeals to have the local educational psychologist assess Brendan kept falling on deaf ears. The school said that there was a twelve to fifteen month waiting list to get an educational psychology assessment, since almost every child in the unit needed one prior to the next year's school placement. So we took the decision to have Brendan's intelligence and cognitive abilities assessed by a private educational psychologist. I realised that I was privileged to be able to afford this.

The educational psychologist put Brendan on par with his peers in terms of intelligence and cognition but said that he was far behind his peers in his social and verbal communications. It was a relief to have the report, because with that on our side, I knew that Brendan would not be put into a special needs school for those with severe learning difficulties. I didn't want this, as I was convinced it would not be in his best interest. At the time the authorities agreed with my insistence that Brendan was functioning quite well, so a specialist autism school was not suggested. I argued that his verbal dyspraxia was far more important than his autism which was light to moderate. Nobody dared to oppose me and tell me I was in denial about the severity of my child's autism.

I wrote many letters and had multiple meetings with the Local Educational Authority and in true tiger-mother style I refused all the suggested schools and insisted he should go instead to a speech and language unit in a local mainstream school. I got him in there, but within a few months it was clear that it was a disaster. Brendan found himself in a class of 20 children, where he was overwhelmed and had regular meltdowns which meant he had to be taken out of the class, kept apart from the other children and given one-to-one attention. The school called me to an urgent meeting one day, in which Brendan's teacher burst into tears because our child was causing her so much stress. They had tried everything to get Brendan involved in the class, they said, but he just couldn't cope. They did not feel that the school was appropriate for Brendan's needs.

With hindsight this was not a surprise. Brendan was the only one in the class with autism, and the teacher had no training in the specialist skills needed to work with children with ASD. I was very calm during the meeting, but deep down, I was very upset. I didn't want to hear that my son was not wanted in the class as he was too disruptive and that the teachers could not cope with him. Luckily Eugene was with me and so was Brendan's speech therapist and the special educational needs (SEN) officer for the local authority.

We conceded that the placement at the speech and language unit in the mainstream school wasn't working and after ten unhappy, stressful months in the mainstream school Brendan was given a place in Abbot's Lea, a very good school for children with ASD, where he started at the age of five. We were lucky to get a place, because the school had a very long waiting list.

Brendan settled happily into Abbot's Lea school. He was given three 20 minute sessions of speech therapy a day from a therapist specifically trained to work with verbal dyspraxia – something I had insisted was included as a necessity in his statement of educational needs and EHCP.

Brendan also had his special AAC device, the Liberator to help him communicate. He was the only child in the school at the time to have one and by the time he reached school he was very competent with it and the teachers had received training on how to use the AAC device effectively.

In his new school Brendan was in a small class with children who had similar needs and he settled well after a month, made friends and began to enjoy school. All the staff and teachers had autism training and the whole school had a level of autism awareness that made the children feel more at ease. For example, they had a quiet sensory room for the children to go to when their sensory processing became too overwhelming. And there were social stories and picture exchange communication cards (PECS) everywhere to help the children who were more visual. The staff would look for all kinds of ways of helping the children to learn.

Brendan also received Occupational therapy (OT) in school. This worked on his sensory processing, with the goal of settling Brendan so that he could focus on lessons in the classroom. Brendan always liked physical activity and motion activities, and he was often allowed to go outside and play on his scooter for five minutes every half hour between lessons, as an outlet for his energy, so that he could concentrate better in the next lesson. He also had a sensory seat cushion on his chair that was filled with gel and had raised circular patterns for tactile stimulation. The aim was to encourage weight-shifting and movement, to allow Brendan to focus during classroom activities and to remain on his chair and not to jump off it so often.

I don't regret going down the wrong track with his choice of schools because it taught me a lot. Acknowledging the full extent of Brendan's educational needs was a process that took time. We are our children's advocates and we have to do what we think is best. It is perhaps inevitable that there will be a few stumbles and mistakes along the way, but they will always have us, their parents, in their corner with their best interests at heart.

Quick Tips

- Make sure that you get your child an individualised Education, Health and Care Plan (EHCP) before they are old enough to start school if possible.
- Contact your local Parent Partnership Services (see Information section at the end of the book) which can provide key information on awareness, rights, independence, choices and inclusion for parents.

- You are your child's advocate, so hold out and fight for what you feel is in your child's best interest – but be willing to listen to what others have to say and to admit when you are wrong too.
- Keep close links with your child's school; get to know teachers, go to meetings and stay involved in decisions about your child's welfare and education.

12

Pushing the Boundaries

We never stopped pushing the boundaries for Brendan. Anything we taught him took much, much longer than it would for a child who did not have autism and we had to find depths of patience and perseverance we didn't know were possible. But we were determined to give him as many skills and abilities as we could and to enable him to connect with others in every way possible. Our concern about Brendan having vital life skills in order to navigate the world around him and to manage in whatever situations his future might bring was greater than the impulse – which we undoubtedly felt at times – to give up.

We taught him to ride a bike. He was uncoordinated and struggled with the concept, but Eugene spent patient hours helping him get used to the pedals, physically moving his feet on them so that he could feel and learn what he needed to do. For a long time he could only cycle the pedals backwards. When finally he wobbled his way for a few metres on his own, I was so proud of him. And he loved it – he had discovered something he could do with purpose and intent. Eventually he became very competent on a bike. And we taught him to rollerblade and to use a skateboard too, Eugene always made sure that Brendan was extremely well-padded before letting him try out a skateboard or rollerblades, and Brendan seemed to enjoy these activities a lot – perhaps because they involved movement. We also bought a huge trampoline with secure netting all around it. Brendan loved it and it was a good way for him to enjoy playing in the garden and to learn to accept other children sharing it with him.

Swimming was a huge success. I mentioned earlier that we discovered, on a trip to Center Parcs when Brendan was two, that he loved the water. After this, with patient determination and persistence on Eugene's part, over the next few years Brendan learned to swim. And we also got him used to the deep end of a pool, so that he would understand that he could stand up in some parts of the pool and not in others. It took many visits to the local swimming pool, but eventually he was completely safe in a pool, he learned to swim well, understood that he couldn't stand up in the deep end and was able to get himself safely in and out. These skills meant a great deal to us, because once they were in place he would always be able to enjoy going for a swim. And it also gave us peace of mind, knowing that he would be safe around swimming pools.

Technology was a success too. By the age of five Brendan knew how to use a laptop or iPad. I introduced him to

Busythings.co.uk, an award-winning website that introduces children to digital learning, the alphabet, phonetics and maths through exploration and games, with high-quality curriculum-linked content that is age-appropriate and fun. Starfall.com is another website that is excellent for teaching children the alphabet through song and games and it aims to teach children reading and comprehension. Brendan had the apps downloaded for both websites and he loved the games he could play there, which also contributed to his learning.

He could also use the remote control for the television. And like many children with autism (and quite a few who do not have it) Brendan could be quite obsessive insisting on watching the TV channels that he was interested in without any regard for anyone else. He would enjoy certain films – or to be more accurate, certain sections of the films, which he soon learned to replay over and over again. The flying whale scene in Fantasia was one that he loved; he would sit and watch it scores of times.

We always set goals – but at the same time we had to be realistic. For example, I was determined that Brendan would learn to independently shower and brush his teeth, dress himself and cut up and eat his food. And he did learn to do all these things. But it took years. There was no point in me setting the goal of him doing all of this by the age of six. But he managed it all by the age of ten. So the goals were fulfilled and it didn't matter that it took a good few years to get there.

We continued to work hard with Brendan on his speaking. At school he was learning expressive speech through Nuffield intensive speech therapy and we worked with this same system at home, to support the work at school.

Both at home and at school we continued to use all kinds of tricks and techniques to help him enunciate words. For example, as part of the Nuffield intensive speech therapy, we had to teach Brendan how to produce certain sounds using his tongue and lips. To get him to place the tip of his tongue to the top of his palate we would place a tiny piece of his favourite barbecue-flavour Pringle on the tip of his tongue and then show him in a mirror so that he could see it. This exercise would eventually help him to produce the 'L' sound.

We would play games like, 'Round and round the garden,' singing and doing movements repetitively. When we got to the last line, 'We all fall... *down*' we would miss out the last word so that Brendan would say it as part of an enjoyable game, although even then it sometimes took him a while to get there, while we all waited patiently mid-game. The idea was to link speech with movement and in this way stimulate speech. Children with autism like to move and swing their hips or rock, using strong movements. So Brendan enjoyed the movements, dancing in a circle, falling down. And while he would not sing all the words, he could manage part of it.

We tried to get Brendan to be an active part of every game. When we played games like chase or pushing him on a swing, he had to start the game by saying, 'Go' – we would wait, often for many minutes until he managed to produce a sound to initiate the action. To start with it didn't sound like 'Go' but just making any sound was a start. We had learned on the courses we took that we needed to take every opportunity to get into Brendan's space and interact with him by finding things that we could do together that he would enjoy.

Another thing we did to encourage him to speak was to put his favourite toys or foods within view but out of his reach, so that he had to ask for them. He could point, gesture, sign, use a PECs picture card or ask verbally, but whatever route he took we would always encourage him towards being verbal as he progressed further on.

We also offered him something in parts – for example sections of his Lego or bits of a snack, so that he had to make multiple requests, one at a time, if he wanted more of it. Or we might offer him foods that we knew he didn't like, so that he would need to use words or signing to indicate, no, enough, all done, or stop.

We learned to continue an activity until he wanted to stop, so that he could verbally end the activity. This encouraged him to speak and also gave him a sense of being able to control something and being listened to – when he said, 'Enough' then we would respond by stopping.

I would often describe what was happening all the time – 'Mummy is running the bath, now Mummy is turning the tap off, Brendan is taking off his clothes, Brendan is getting in the bath,' and so on. The emphasis was on helping him to understand words, and to see a routine broken down into small parts, making it easier to manage.

Repetition was, and is, the key. Brendan would go through the daily routines hearing the same words over and over again, helping him to remember them as well as to enjoy the security of predictable routine. It meant us slowing things down, taking him through each stage and this wasn't always easy when we had so much to fit into a day, but we stuck as rigidly as we could to the same way of doing things.

We never pressured Brendan to talk, instead we gave him the words, the pictures, the signs and the opportunities and let him find his way towards actually using the words.

We tried to offer Brendan choices as often as possible. We began with very simple choices, between two things he could see – one he liked, one he disliked, holding them up and saying, 'Brendan do you want the banana or the apple?' To get the apple he would need to indicate his choice. And gradually he moved from pointing or holding up a picture, to using the word.

By the age of seven, two years after starting at his special school, Brendan was talking so well that he was able to manage without his AAC tablet, the Liberator.

This was a major achievement, something we had been told he might never manage and a source of huge joy and relief for us. Thankfully it was clear that, far from holding him back as some experts had initially suggested; the system of picture cards (PECS) and then the AAC Liberator had helped him learn to speak. The Nuffield speech therapy was also crucial in helping Brendan develop the speech sounds in a step-by-step approach.

His speech was not, and still is not, perfect. He could say many words, but could not always make himself understood by saying them clearly enough. At home we understand him well, but out and about he sometimes – though certainly not always – needs an interpreter. An iPad helps him to locate words or objects when he is stuck, and we continue to work with him on his speaking.

Without access to the three systems we used – PECS cards, the Liberator and the Nuffield Speech Programme that his speech therapists implemented – Brendan would not be speaking. It took a great deal of hard work from all of us to help him learn to form and express the sounds he needed.

His vocabulary grew to be extensive. But his speech was, and is, largely functional; he will ask for what he wants, or tell us what he is doing or what he likes. He can also answer simple questions like, 'Did you do drawing today?' or 'Did you go to the shop today?' We encourage him to tell the story of his day at school.

He has learned social communications at school as part of the life skills curriculum. Every week he and his classmates make a grocery and shopping list and go to the shop. They learn how to pay and how to order at a cafe.

We still use Social Stories to depict any social situation that Brendan may encounter, especially a new one. Many people with autism have an impairment of social understanding and the ability to think in ways necessary for appropriate social interaction. We have, over the years, produced social stories for Brendan when he was going to the doctor, the dentist, going on an aeroplane or to the zoo. It helped Brendan to understand the environment and the social situation and to have more appropriate behaviours and fewer anxieties.

We use a three step approach:

- First, read Brendan the social story of going to the doctor
- Second, concentrate on the pictures and the environment of the hospital and clinic and discuss with Brendan what to expect. Allow him to ask questions
- Third, act out the behaviours through role plays such as listening to his chest, opening his mouth, checking his temperature

Brendan didn't just learn to speak, he also learned to sing. I will never forget the day when, driving along in the car with 10 year-old Brendan, he began to sing along to Justin Bieber's 'Baby, Baby'. It was a lovely moment and it was a surprise because he must have heard the song on the CD hundreds of times without making a sound, and then all of a sudden he came out with it, he knew the tune and the words!

He hasn't yet extended to conversational language, which is our goal for him. I'd like him to be able to give an account of something that happened, telling the story – that's what we are gradually moving towards.

Routine has always been at the centre of our lives with Brendan. He needs routine to try to make sense of the world that, to him, must seem so chaotic and overwhelming. We have routines for getting up and getting ready for school, for meals, for leaving the house, arriving home, bath time and bedtime.

All these routines, and many more, were introduced to him with pictures and with us taking the actions to show him, while encouraging him to play a part and to take a turn. Every now and then we would introduce something new into a routine, and perhaps comment on it, as a way of encouraging his participation and encouraging him to accept new elements too.

We've always used routines for any kind of outing or trip, creating picture boards to tell him what would happen so that he could understand and be prepared. But we did realise that, crucial as routine and predictability is to someone with ASD, it is also vital, occasionally, to include a little disorder or 'chaos' now and then, to help them cope when things don't go to plan.

Inevitably sometimes things will go wrong. And when I read about a boy with ASD who took his own life when a school trip he had been looking forward to for months and preparing for was suddenly cancelled, I was alarmed and devastated. This boy felt so unable to deal with change that he had no idea how to cope. It was terribly sad and I didn't want that to happen to Brendan, so we began to introduce some variation for him, making his world less structured from time to time. For instance we would take him somewhere unfamiliar without first preparing him by reading him a story about it or creating a PECS card sequence. Or we would change the plan, in a small way, for what we were going to do on a non-school day. I might say to him, 'Darren has a cold so we can't go swimming, but we will go to the shops instead'.

As a parent, I wanted for Brendan to be able to cope with breaks in the routine and to manage his discomfort around change while we were there to support him, so that when, inevitably, there was change later on in his life, he would be better able to cope with it.

It was actually nice for us because it meant there was a small window for impromptu or unplanned things – on one occasion we took him to a pantomime of the Ice Queen at the Edinburgh Fringe Festival without first preparing him.

Of course Brendan didn't like this at all, he would often have a huge meltdown, screaming and throwing himself about. But as time has gone on he has gotten better at accepting change and that is reassuring.

Quick Tips

- Use routines as the mainstay of your child's day but, over time, introduce breaks in the routine to allow your child to cope with change.
- Be prepared to go over and over the things you are teaching your child. It may take a long time for him or her to learn something new.
- Give your child several warnings and visual or verbal cues about what is going to happen, even something as simple as bedtime.
- Use pictures and social stories to prepare your child for something new.
- Don't be afraid to push the boundaries, if you don't, how will you know what your child is capable of?
- Set goals, be consistent with your approach and be realistic about the time they may take to achieve.

13

Sensory Issues

Children diagnosed with Autistic Spectrum Disorder (ASD) often have difficulty processing everyday sensory information. Any of their senses may be over-or under-sensitive, or both, at different times.

These sensory issues often affect their behaviour and can have a profound effect on their everyday life, not only disrupting a child's ability to learn in school and form friendships, but having a profound impact on family life.

Brendan had severe difficulties processing everyday sensory information in all of his senses, from noise, to touch, to smells, sounds and tastes.

When he was very small we didn't understand this, and looking back I feel sad thinking of how hard it must have been for him. Once we had his ASD diagnosis we soon learned about the sensory issues that so often go with it and it didn't take long to realise that much of Brendan's distress, his shouting, jumping up and down, hurling himself about and inability to sit or keep still, was down to his sensory distress and the anxiety that arose from it.

He could not listen to certain music or sounds from the television. Noises which often mean nothing to the rest of us seemed to cause him pain and distress. He would put his hands over his ears and shout until we switched it off. Even turning the sound down was often not enough.

We have worked hard to try to desensitise him and to some extent it has worked. We have repeated the sounds he dislikes while distracting him with something he likes, like a game in the iPad. And his tolerance has increased, although many sounds still bother him. These sounds can be of a certain pitch or note and do not necessarily have to be loud. I still find it hard to comprehend that he can be so sensitive to certain sounds and not others. This is made more complicated by the fact that there does not appear to be any patterns to the sounds that he finds distressing, so it can be very hard to predict what will or will not upset him.

Certain clothes would also be unbearable to him, he would tear them off as if they were burning his skin. Man-made fabrics troubled him most, and he also hated labels inside clothing. While these can be annoying at times for most of us, for Brendan they were impossible to stand.

We were able to make sure that he had clothing in fabrics he liked. But some things are far less easy to change or negotiate. The areas that probably gave us the most trouble were practical physical routines that have to be navigated – cleaning teeth and cutting hair and nails. Brendan absolutely hated all of them.

When it was time to brush his teeth he would shut his mouth – or open it and scream. The mouth is one of the most sensitive areas of the body, so for Brendan the process of teeth brushing felt intolerable. It was hard to get a toothbrush near his mouth. When he was a toddler I spent many hours preparing him, reading stories about teeth brushing and making reward charts for him. I started using a soft bristle brush and a vibrating toothbrush with a timer, so that he would know exactly how long he had to do it for, and bit by bit we got there, but it took years before he could.

Visits to the dentist were incredibly difficult. We did our best to prepare him, starting a week before the appointment, reading him stories like 'Sensitive Sam goes to the Dentist' and 'Topsy and Tim Go to the Dentist'. We would explain to him with pictures exactly what would happen, that he would sit in the chair and need to lean back and open his mouth wide and keep it open so that the dentist can look inside and so on.

Despite all the preparation, once we got to the dentist Brendan would shut his mouth tightly and resist any attempt to get him to open his mouth. There would often be a full-scale meltdown, his arms and legs flailing as the nurse or dentist attempted to coax him into opening his mouth wide.

We were very lucky in being able to go to a special needs dental clinic locally, where the staff were experienced with children like Brendan and were patient and kind. We didn't need to explain his behaviour or apologise, and that helped us all a lot. It isn't always possible to find a dentist like this, but it's worth asking around to see if there is one in your local area.

We always promised a reward for him to look forward to if the visit went well – usually a small toy or magazine that he liked. He was also allowed to hold a toy while the dentist was working – it acted as a comforter for him and helped to stop him from thrashing his hands around. And somehow, with all of these things in place, he got through the visit and had his check-up.

It was worse if he had a toothache. He didn't like his mouth being prodded or touched at the best of times, but when he was in pain he was even more reluctant – he had no idea the dentist was there to help. His fear and anxiety would spiral and our stress levels would soar. We didn't want to distress him, but his toothache had to be treated.

At one point Brendan developed a tooth abscess. His face became swollen and he was clearly in a lot of pain and screaming his head off. We took him to hospital but no-one could persuade him to open his mouth. Even his adored Pringles didn't work, so he had to be put under a general anaesthetic. He had an impacted molar which had to be removed. He was put onto intravenous antibiotics and would normally have had to stay in hospital for five days, but as it would have been completely impossible to keep him in a hospital bed, we took him home and a wonderful children's nursing service helped us to treat him at home.

Dentist visits were something we all dreaded for several years. Gradually Brendan's baby teeth fell out and the adult ones came in and luckily he didn't have serious problems or need a brace.

We also had to teach him to floss his teeth, as dental hygienists recommended this. Once again we got through it with preparation, planning, rewards and perseverance. As with many other things, Brendan soon realised that we were not going to give up or stop, so he had to learn to accept it.

Another huge milestone was going to the barber. Even brushing Brendan's hair distressed him, so we knew that getting it cut was going to be extremely challenging. We contacted many barbers, asking them if we could bring him in, but when we warned them that he might well be screaming they turned us down. We eventually found a kind barber who agreed to help and he was wonderful. He really understood autism and he would cut Brendan's hair very quickly, distracting him with a toy and tolerating his shouts of disapproval. Again we would prepare Brendan carefully, but no amount of preparation made the visit easy.

When we moved home a few years later we continued to travel the 20 miles back to see this barber, because no-one else could cut Brendan's hair, until eventually Eugene took over the job and did it at home, making it far less stressful for Brendan.

Because of his sensory issues Brendan jumped around a lot and it was hard to get him to keep still for long enough to eat. So we decided to consult an occupational therapist for ideas on how we might help him. She suggested we put a sand vest on him. This is like a waistcoat with pockets containing tiny bags of sand to weigh him down. Sportsmen and women often use them in training to give them an additional challenge.

The sand vest worked really well – we got a very small one that wasn't very heavy, and the additional weight seemed to ground Brendan enough to reduce his jumping, so we used it for mealtimes and at other times when we particularly needed him to keep still.

We kept egg timers all over the house. They are very visual and they gave Brendan a perception of time, which is otherwise so hard to quantify. A two-minute timer could be used for brushing teeth, and other activities could be divided into units of two minutes. We also had a five-and ten-minute timer for activities like homework of a task on the TEACCH programme.

At times we learned to ignore his meltdowns, simply allowing him time to calm down. But at other times, when we needed him to stop and concentrate on a task, we would take a toy away from him. Eugene would, very occasionally, throw things in the bin, so that Brendan would understand that he wouldn't see them again. After that if we said it would go in the bin Brendan knew what it meant. But usually we would put the toy in the naughty box. Brendan could earn it back again by calming down and doing what he needed to do.

We haven't often relied on time out as a consequence. The concept of putting him in a separate room, or on a 'naughty step', is one we have used carefully because it takes Brendan away from what is going on, which is often just what he wants. Say, for instance, he was hitting one of us because he didn't want to make his bed. Giving him time out would give him what he wanted – to avoid the task. So we would try to keep him engaged and at the same time look for a way to avoid his need to hit (which might be because he felt overwhelmed by the task). In a lot of cases helping him with it, and breaking it down into small steps, was the key. And we would make sure that he completed the final action in the routine, for instance putting the pillow back in place.

Sleep continued to be an issue; Brendan never slept through the night and he still doesn't. We considered using sleep aids, such as melatonin, but the evidence that it works is not conclusive and we didn't like the idea of giving him an unnecessary drug.

Whereas when he was younger we always went into his room when he shouted in the night, as he grew older we began getting up less often. We had taught him to stay in his room, and as long as he does that we can leave him to fall asleep again on his own.

For us consistency plus straightforward rules and techniques applied over and over again over a long period of time has been the key to bringing about gradual change in the most challenging aspects of Brendan's behaviour. Patience and persistence are really virtues we developed and honed over time.

The courses we attended and the lessons we learned also taught us to grasp opportunities to engage with Brendan and to be as creative as possible in finding ways to engage. We often used songs and games to teach Brendan new skills or to help him to tolerate certain activities.

There is no doubt that the sensory issues have made an enormous impact on our lives. It is impossible for someone who doesn't live with autism to imagine how much difference the extra sensitivity makes to every aspect of life. I know that research into sensory issues in autism is still underway and I am hopeful that in the near future progress will be made in finding ways to help those with ASD and their families with this very tough aspect of the condition.

Quick Tips

- Your child may be overwhelmed by sensory experiences all day. By understanding their difficulties, you can provide the right sensory experience and environment at home or school, which will make a huge difference to your child's life.
- A sand-vest may help your child to feel calmer and more grounded.
- Play is essential in order to learn new skills, so use books, cards, songs and games to teach your child and help them develop sensory processing abilities and skills.
- The more independent your child, the easier life will be. So persist in teaching them to manage tasks for themselves.
- Look for dentists and hairdressers who are autism aware and perhaps educate them.

14

Three Children and a Dog

In December 2009 we had our third child – a little girl we called Corinne. I was so delighted to have a little girl, I felt our family was now complete.

Of course we worried about whether she would have problems. We had two special needs boys and at that point we hadn't yet had the hearing loss diagnosis for Darren, we still didn't know why he wasn't speaking. So the decision to go ahead and have a third was brave, and in some eyes foolish. But it was a plan I had long held dear, to have three children. I rarely abandoned a plan once I had it planted firmly in my head.

I did worry, at one point, that I may have unconsciously conceived Corinne to relieve the burden on Darren of having a brother with autism. I don't know whether there was a grain of truth in that. I do think that in future years it will help that there are two of them to look out for

Brendan. But at the same time, I really did always want a third child!

During the pregnancy I had all kinds of checks including counselling with the obstetrician. I had a very good obstetrician who said that there was an extremely low chance of having either autism or placenta praevia more than once. But in the end I think what prevailed was sheer optimism and the belief that, whatever happened, the siblings would be good for one another.

Although there was a low chance of repeating previous problems, there were still concerns when I was pregnant with Corinne. I was once again diagnosed with placenta praevia and at one point it was feared that I might also have placenta accreta, a medical condition in which the placenta attaches itself to the uterine wall, risking heavy bleeding during a vaginal delivery and with it potential blood transfusion or even hysterectomy. For this reason I was given another caesarean, and Corinne was born early, at 32 weeks. Although she was small, being eight weeks before her due date, Corinne appeared healthy. But wary of conditions which can emerge within the first few weeks, we kept a very close eye on her. It was soon clear, though, that she was absolutely fine and this was a joy for us, reminding us that life – and having children – is such a lottery.

With the addition of a third baby we had three children under five – a handful under any circumstances. Luckily we had a wonderful au pair, Anna. She came from the Philippines but had settled in the Wirral with her English husband. She had joined us after Theresa left and she ended up staying with us for eight years – the children loved her very much and she became part of our family. I always feel incredibly blessed to have known Anna.

We always wanted our three children to be close to one another, so we kept them in the same room together and did things as a family, including all three in every outing and family event. We didn't want Corinne and Darren to think of Brendan as in any way different or separate from themselves, but simply as the brother they loved and would always look after.

Despite our good intentions, Brendan's initial reaction to the arrival of Corinne was to completely ignore her, not only when she first arrived home from hospital, but for a long time afterwards, just as he had with Darren. He refused to even look into the Moses basket and say hello to her. As far as he was concerned this new person in the house was totally irrelevant and uninteresting, unless she was crying, in which case he put his hands over his ears and fled, or became distressed too. He liked order, and Corinne's arrival disrupted the order of the house. We worked very hard, and patiently, to show Brendan who Corinne was, to involve him in her care and to bring the three children together in the household, as one harmonious unit.

Before Corinne was born, we had tried to prepare Brendan for the arrival of his baby sister. We had a children's story book called The New Baby, by Anne Civardi, published by Usborne books. I read the story to him several times, but Brendan didn't seem to like the book and would prefer to choose other books to read. I thought he just couldn't understand the concept of the new baby, until one day I arrived home from work to find that Brendan had used colouring pencils to scratch out all the pictures of the baby in the New Baby book. It occurred to me then that he may have understood perfectly well what we were telling him and simply not liked the idea of having a new baby in the house.

When Darren began crawling, at ten months old, Brendan, not yet three, would frequently become distressed, shouting and screaming as Darren, keen to explore his new ability to get around, crawled towards Brendan's careful line-up of Thomas the Tank Engine trains or his Hotwheel cars. It had taken quite some time to get him used to Darren, and it was the same with his baby sister.

Corinne joined the boys in their room, even though initially Brendan's night-waking woke her, as it had with Darren (who now slept pretty soundly through it all) and her crying woke Brendan in turn. We wanted them to get used to one another, and in time, they did.

Thankfully, Corinne passed all her milestones and began talking early, as girls often do. She had no hearing problem and no sign of ASD, although she did develop asthma and all three children have a severe allergy to peanuts and have to carry epi-pens (epinephrine injection) to antidote their reaction should they accidentally ingest any peanut. We discovered that Brendan had this allergy when he was very small, he was hospitalised twice, and after that, we tested the other two as babies and found that they had it too.

As two working parents in demanding jobs, managing three young children, one of them with ASD, even with Anna's help, was a tough challenge. We needed routines, boundaries and clear, simple rules. We wanted the family to be a cohesive unit, all of us doing things together, with Brendan very much a part of that.

One of our big concerns was that Brendan still had no sense of danger. And as he grew a little older he began mimicking superheroes – standing on the kitchen worktops and, once, getting onto the banister at the top of the stairs. I almost had a heart attack when I saw him, I didn't know whether he was planning to jump or not. I had to coax him down as calmly as possible.

After that there was a clear rule that no-one stood on the banister or kitchen worktops and there was strictly no jumping from them. I was also afraid that Darren and Corinne may mimic Brendan's dangerous behaviours.

We decided on our house rules carefully and once they were in place there were no exceptions. Eugene, Anna and I were consistent. That was the only way any of the children, but particularly Brendan, would know that we meant it.

We created a reward system with pasta shells when the children were old enough to understand the system. The children could earn some pasta shells for good behaviour like cleaning teeth for two minutes, doing homework or helping with household chores.

We taught them all basic skills like washing up the dishes, putting the dirty laundry in the washing machine and hanging the laundry to dry. Brendan hated doing chores as much as his brother and sister. Children with autism are no different when it comes to chores, but such skills are necessary and fundamental if there was to be a chance that he could live independently.

Luckily they didn't hate every single chore; they all seemed to love mopping floors, and that would earn them five shells. Their pasta shells could then be exchanged for something they wanted. For instance playing video games – 5 pasta shells bought an hour on the iPad. Or 10 shells for a small Lego toy. Eugene would buy them and put them on a shelf where the children could see them, as an incentive for them to save their shells. From the start Darren was very good at saving his shells in exchange for bigger rewards, while Corinne and Brendan would spend their shells straight away on iPad or TV time. They soon learned the value of patience in saving for bigger rewards.

Whoever finished their meal first also got a shell, but we had to exclude Darren from this after some time because he always finished first, while the other two would dawdle over their food for ages if left to it. This was an example of a rule not always being the same for all of them, and we would sometime change rules which they always accepted.

For Brendan the system was very important, he liked to exchange his shells for time on the iPad or TV, and it was important for him to see that his siblings shared the same system and the same rules.

All rules are broken from time to time, so once a rule was created, it was important for us to set the consequences when the rule was broken. All the children knew that breaking rules meant the removal of some of their pasta shells, or time out from a chosen activity.

Time out meant the quiet room. A naughty step never worked – Brendan would not stay there – so it had to be a room. We used a spare office room and removed all toys or distractions and, as a guideline, we would give the children one minute of time out for every year of their age. So at five years old, Brendan would have five minutes of time out. This was a good way of making it clear to him, and to the others, that there was a consequence for unacceptable behaviour. And in Brendan's case, if he was having a meltdown, removing him from anything too stimulating (such as the TV or the computer) would help him to calm down.

We always worked hard to give the children equal amounts of attention, and time on their own with each parent. As Darren and Corinne grew a little older we read them books about having a brother with autism. Both of them had gone through phases of doing things to make Brendan scream (all too easy) or of competing with him for attention by screaming or playing up themselves. But Brendan could not retaliate, and we needed them to understand this, and that distressing him in any way was not OK. We have read them quite a few books available like My brother has autism by Debbie Jaeger, My brother is autistic by Jennifer Moore-Mallinos and My brother is different by Louise Gorrod and Becci Carver.

Darren and Corinne would, on many occasions, become very frustrated with Brendan's rigid behaviour patterns – such as watching the same film scene over and over again, and his refusal to listen, share or negotiate.

Situations like this brought home to us how much a diagnosis of autism for one child affects the whole family. All the social interactions have to be managed; the frustrations of the other children (and the parents) and the inability of the child with autism to see or understand how anyone else is feeling or what they want.

We always tried to interest Brendan in toys that his siblings were playing with, and to encourage them to play together. We had to abandon board games as, even after ten years of trying, Brendan couldn't manage them, but he learned to love other games – an egg hunt, hide and seek and tag became our favourites.

Both Darren and Corinne have had to accept that there are times they will feel embarrassed or upset by Brendan's behaviour. Their friends might comment or give Brendan funny looks and it will be uncomfortable for them, but they are protective of Brendan and will stand up for their brother.

On one occasion, when we were shopping in Tesco, Darren, then aged ten, became upset by Brendan who was shouting and said to him, 'Why do you have to shout and flap your hands like that?' He was clearly embarrassed about being out with his brother. I understood, but I wasn't going to accept it. I spoke to Darren later, and said I was disappointed in him because he knew that Brendan could not help his behaviour. Darren apologised and said he understood but he explained that sometimes, when his brother frustrated him, he can't help himself. That day, after we had talked, Darren sat down and wrote a poem which beautifully expressed his feelings for his brother.

My brother has autism
And I really should know
He makes me feel like a volcano
Which is just about to explode!

I know I shouldn't blame him
But I don't know what to do!
He's like a bull in a china shop,
So tell, me, what should I do?

(Sigh) I know it's not his fault
He isn't one to blame
He tries his best, and tries again
And again and again and again!

So I love my brother Brendan
And he loves me too
No matter how irritating he is,
We're brothers, me and you

We have felt concerned that Darren has had to grow up quickly, as his brother's 'older' sibling, rather than being the younger. But there is no way round it, we could not put any of the children in bubble-wrap, we had to cope with the hand we were dealt. We do make sure that Darren and Corinne have time with their own friends and doing their own activities – they both get invited to many parties and to friends' houses and that gives them a little time away.

We do our best to let our children bond as much as possible through outings, activities and even PlayStation games! We got them to play Nintendo SnipperClips which is a fantastic two-player cooperative family game in which two or more players control colourful paper figures called Snip and Clip. Each player has to communicate with the other player so that together they snip each other into shapes to solve a variety of puzzles and go on to the next level. This game provided an excellent way for Brendan, with either Darren or Corinne to communicate and talk to one another, working together to complete the levels in the game.

I am hugely thankful that Darren and Corinne have grown to understand their brother and his autism, and their understanding, patience and love for him grow deeper with the passing years.

The next addition to our household, after a lot of careful deliberation and research, was Muffin the dog.

I had never had a pet as a child and was very apprehensive about taking on another responsibility, but I loved the idea of the children having one. And I had read about autism support dogs in the States and the difference they make to children with ASD. For some of these children, a dog helps with positive changes in behaviour and gives them comfort and companionship. I watched video clips of ASD support dogs trained to calm a child with autism down; even weighing the child down during a meltdown, and I wondered if that might help Brendan and if a dog would be bonding for all the children.

Initially I went to a company in Northern Ireland called Autism Support Dogs UK that promised to provide a fully-trained autism dog, but the company was later exposed in 2016 as a fraud before we got a dog, and we were left wondering what to do.

There are other companies, reputable ones, that train autism support dogs, but they are few and far between. There is a very long waiting list and the dogs are often for children aged 3 – 10 years. By this time Brendan was 11, and too old anyway, so after much debate, we decided we would simply have a family pet dog and we bought a puppy from an established breeder. We travelled all the way to Wales to see the breeder and his dogs.

Muffin is a poodle/bichon-frise mix. These dogs are hypo allergenic and they don't shed their fur. Perfect for us with Corinne's asthma, Brendan's eczema and the children's nut allergies. He is an adorable, fluffy little dog and he has fitted in very well, we all love him – although like all puppies, he started out by chewing everything in sight, much to the children's consternation (if it was their toy he chewed) and amusement (if it was someone else's toy that he chewed).

Brendan was wary at first – he had run a mile from our good friends' Jack Russell and he wasn't too keen on having one of these strange creatures that was always jumping at him or barking in the house. Six months after Muffin's arrival, Brendan was still shouting a lot every time Muffin jumped at him, so I asked him if he wanted Muffin to go to live with a friend of ours as company for her dog. Brendan shouted out in protest to say that he didn't want Muffin to go. It took some time for him to calm down as he became anxious at the thought of Muffin leaving us. We realised then that Brendan truly considered Muffin to be part of the family, even if he did find Muffin annoying.

Over time, Eugene and I got Brendan to hold the lead and help walk Muffin around the garden and within eight months he became used to Muffin and would give him a treat, or throw a ball for him. It is our hope that, in living with a dog, Brendan will find a companion he can trust and love. When eventually Darren and Corinne grow up and leave home to live their own lives, it comforts me to think that Brendan will still have Muffin for company.

Quick Tips

- A reward system can be a powerful learning tool for your child.
- Encourage close relationships with siblings and cousins who grow up with a child with autism, they will simply accept her or him for who they are and that is a source of real joy.
- Your child with autism can learn to share with their siblings and can be given the same fair reward system and rules.
- Please consider having a pet carefully as it is a big responsibility and pets should be part of the family should you choose to have one.
- Pets can be great for all children – with or without autism.
- Aim to give all children in the family equal amounts of your time and remember the impact on your other children of growing up with a sibling with autism.
- Manage negative feelings by communicating in a non-judgemental way.

15

Out and About

Brendan hated new environments, but at every opportunity we would take him out into different settings. We wanted him to be able to accept change and new places, to improve his social skills and to follow our instructions in managing himself in a place that was unfamiliar to him.

We also wanted to feel that, as a family, we could go out and about, to nice restaurants, cinemas and on holiday. We didn't want to feel that we had to stay at home all the time, afraid to take Brendan out. So it was a question of choosing where we went and preparing well.

We soon realised that one of us could not take all three children out that easily. It was just too much to handle if Brendan had a meltdown. Eugene or I could manage two children on our own, but for all three to go anywhere it took two of us to manage.

As unfamiliar environments caused Brendan great

distress, for anything we planned he needed careful preparation and advance warning. We had to create a picture board telling him the story of what we would do, as well as telling him stories about it and reminding him of it every day for several days before we actually went anywhere.

This was always true for anything we did. Even at home, Brendan needed ample notice that any event was going to happen. Bedtime, for instance, despite being a totally familiar ritual, would be signaled to him ten minutes before, then five minutes, using the timers to show him how long he had and after that we would warn him verbally too. For going out somewhere, we needed proportionately more notice and preparation.

Restaurants were always difficult. If he didn't like the place, Brendan would slam his hands on the table, or suddenly jump, often banging his head on a table or wall in the process. He might also scream, flap his hands, hold his hands over his ears, bite himself, pinch himself or lash out at others. While any or all of these things were going on, people at nearby tables would look angrily over at us, wondering why we couldn't control our misbehaving child. It was incredibly stressful and difficult to ignore their glaring looks.

Meanwhile Eugene and I would be telling Corinne and Darren to keep quiet and be calm, while also trying to calm Brendan down. Sometimes we just had to get up and leave. We learned to go to places with no loud music playing and with fewer customers. But even then, it was hard.

I always found other people's unkind reactions very difficult to take. And it wasn't much easier if Brendan ended up having a meltdown in public and people tried to help. Anyone attempting to talk to Brendan or, worse still, touch him would only make him worse. Few people showed understanding that this was a child with autism. If we didn't go to restaurants sometimes, how could we ever teach Brendan to manage them? We didn't want to hide him at home, and we shouldn't have to.

When I discovered autism awareness cards through further research, it helped me find a way to turn something negative to a more positive approach. These are simply worded cards that you can hand out to anyone who seems to be taking an interest, positive or negative, when your child is attracting attention in public.

There are all kinds of cards available over the internet. I chose a card with the following message, in English, Spanish, French and German:

Our child has autism. He is not being naughty and we are not bad parents for not reprimanding him. Children with autism find it hard to cope with everyday situations. Please be patient.

For sources of cards such as these see the Information Section at the end of the book.

Being able to show this card to people around us made a difference, they would look at it and nod in understanding and give us some space to deal with Brendan. And gradually, as we regularly took him out, Brendan got a little more used to new situations so that today he is calm and well-behaved most of the time in a restaurant. Of course he can still have a meltdown, he is never completely predictable, but these days I no longer feel like a bad mother, or get embarrassed if he does. I simply deal with it, and hand the card to anyone who is watching.

When Brendan was five and I was pregnant for the third time, we took him to Disneyland in Paris with Darren who was then three. We had a special disabled pass because of Brendan's autism, but I felt bad skipping the queues and wanted Brendan to learn how to stand in line and wait, so mostly that's what we did. There were times he really could not manage to wait in a very long queue and had meltdowns and when this happened we would give in and go to the fast pass queue, but I felt guilty every time we did this. Eugene didn't have any issues with using the disabled pass as to him, it enabled giving Brendan a more positive experience without having to queue. The trip to Disneyland was a success, Brendan loved the small, small world ride and we went on it at least 10 times, with Brendan shouting in delight with the music as we rode along on the boat. He was a bit scared of the people in large, furry animal costumes, but eventually he was able to give them a hug and he absolutely loved the fireworks at the end. It was a real joy for us to see him so happy.

Taking him to the cinema was another challenge. We first took him to see Wall-E, a children's science fiction film about a robot that we thought he would like. Again we prepared him, taking him to Disney stores to see the merchandise for the film, and showing him previews of the film. But nothing could really prepare him for the size of the screen or the noise of the film. He was so distressed, shouting and jumping off his seat that people mumbled and stared at us, and in the end we had to leave halfway through.

These occasions always upset me a great deal; I couldn't help feeling like a bad parent as I ran the gamut of angry faces. A little kindness or thoughtfulness makes all the difference; on one occasion when we took Brendan to a Mad Max science show, a smaller audience and Brendan was doing his usual stimming, flapping, and bursts of shouting (in delight). I was very uncomfortable and explained loudly to the presenter he had autism.

She turned to the whole audience and said, 'We have a little boy with autism here who is having a lot of fun and I hope you will all make him feel comfortable'. Everyone clapped and she invited Brendan up on stage to help her with the experiments. I almost burst into tears; this was my first experience of bringing him to a public place and actually feeling welcomed, rather than having to be constantly apologetic for the disruptions he made. It was such a positive experience and it made me realise that in the right circumstances taking Brendan out was fine, we just needed supportive and considerate people who would accept that Brendan couldn't control himself as other children could.

After that first attempt to take him to the cinema we didn't feel able to take him back for another four years, until we heard that autism-friendly screenings were available. This was a fantastic breakthrough, which meant that we could take all three children and enjoy a film together.

These screenings, currently available at over 250 cinemas in the UK, are on certain Sunday mornings. Family-friendly films are shown and adjustments are made for sensory sensitivities. These include keeping low lights on, no trailers, the sound lowered to a softer level and a much more relaxed atmosphere, so that no-one minds a child making a noise or getting up and down. You can bring food and drink and sit where you like and the staff are trained in autism awareness. These screenings are organised by Dimensions, an organisation that provides research-based, outcomes-focused services for people with learning disabilities and autism. They work with several of the major screening chains, including Odeon, Vue Cinemas and Cineworld.

Holidays were an even bigger challenge. But Eugene and I decided that we all needed a holiday every summer, to give us a change of scene and to explore the world a little. We kept them pretty safe – going most often to Center Parcs or to Scotland or other UK destinations. We would go in the family car, which was familiar to him, and would take time to settle him into wherever we were staying.

We used to worry a lot about Brendan wandering off, and we always kept him in sight. When he was younger, we had a child lead attached to him so he couldn't wander far. As he got older, I didn't feel comfortable using those leads and would hold his hands or ensure he was always with us nearby. Then one day, when he was eight and we were at Center Parcs, we lost him when we were browsing some shops in an enclosed building. It was a heart-pounding moment, the first time I could remember that neither Eugene nor I could see him. We were frantic and searching everywhere for what felt like many minutes, and I was moments away from being in a state of panic when suddenly we heard Brendan calling out, 'Mummy! Papa!' His voice was so loud that we instantly recognised his voice and shouted back to him. We found him close by and it was then that we realised that if he couldn't see us he would shout for us, which was so reassuring.

On a trip round Scotland when Brendan was 12, we went to see an exhibition about the Loch Ness monster. While watching a video about the Loch Ness monster in an enclosed dark room, a teenage boy hissed 'shush' at Brendan three times because Brendan was making some sounds and stimming, while the boy's parents stood by and did nothing. I almost lost my temper with the boy and was deeply disappointed that his parents did nothing and appeared to condone this rude behaviour. It was so obvious that Brendan was a special needs child as he was stimming and his speech was not quite normal. People who don't judge or glare, and who offer a kind word, make a world of difference.

This wasn't a one-off. Over the years Brendan has been excluded from play areas, swimming classes and drama classes because of the inability of others to understand autism needs. That's why I am passionate about advancing autism awareness. I have been hurt many times over the years by people's callous remarks and assumption that we were bad parents. I am very open about Brendan's autism because I believe that with knowledge and better understanding of autism will come greater compassion and understanding, and more inclusion of people with autism into everyday activities.

We enjoyed skiing and wanted all the children to learn how to ski. Brendan was eleven the first time we took him to the ski slopes and he would scream for hours every day when he first tried on the skis. Corinne and Darren were able to join the ski school but Brendan was not allowed due to his inability to converse and listen to instructions as part of a group. So we had to hire a special disability ski instructor for him. It took us many trips before he became comfortable on the ski slopes, but he did get there, and today he skis competently and rather enjoys it.

Taking Brendan in a plane, and even through the airport, for holidays is often a challenge. I was pleased that Manchester and Liverpool airports had an autism-friendly initiative and if we gave early notice and filled in the forms, we were sent an autism bracelet so that Brendan could go through the fast pass channel and avoid the long queues. He would refuse to remove his shoes going through the security checks, but the staff were understanding and they would allow him to pass through with his shoes on and check him over using the hand-held security device.

Once in the aeroplane, Brendan would be allowed to explore and we would try to distract him with the iPad or tablet. On the longer journeys sleep was an issue. Brendan would be tired, but he couldn't sleep unless he was allowed to lie flat, and we had to explain that he couldn't do this on a plane. We would try to lie him down with his legs over one of us and his head on the other so that he could sleep.

Every couple of years we would go to visit our families in

Malaysia, and it was often hard initially. It was bad enough in England, where we had to listen to people telling us how well their children were doing, or watch as time and again Brendan was not invited to a class birthday party. But when we went back to Malaysia it always felt much worse.

Our immediate families, especially my mother who had cared for Brendan as a baby, were kind and understanding. But there the culture is still one that sends three year-olds to speed-reading classes, that trains small children in mental maths and music and that is strongly competitive and achievement-based.

In the early years, many of those we encountered simply didn't understand what autism was, and well-meaning friends and relatives would send us a stream of messages about new 'cures' and 'therapies'. Many believed that Brendan would grow out of it and be 'cured', or he simply needed the right approach. Much as I love the country of my birth, the visits home grew increasingly painful.

One of the most important things for us was enabling Brendan to join in with things at school, especially outings and trips. His first ever school trip was to Butlins when he was eight years old. Contemplating this week-long trip I was very anxious before the trip as I couldn't believe the teachers would take on such a big responsibility. Who would help him shower, help him after toileting or manage if he wet the bed at night? But they assured me that they would deal with all of it, for Brendan and for the other children. I made sure all his routines were discussed and written down for his teacher, who shared the room with him. He had his favourite teddy to take with him and everything was carefully labelled in his suitcase.

The teachers asked me not to ring them or check up on him, and promised they would let me know if there was the slightest problem. I hadn't realised how hard it would be letting him go – I was so used to being with him all the time I wasn't at work, and to going through his routines with him. But it was nice to have some time with Darren and Corinne while he was away, and to my amazement Brendan loved the trip and came home happy at the end of it.

Teaching Brendan to cope with outings, visits and holidays has given him, and us, a new level of freedom that means a great deal and that opens up possibilities for the future.

Quick Tips

- Don't be afraid to take your child out and about. Give them the opportunity to experience different environments. They have just as much right as others to enjoy outings.
- Don't feel guilty if others comment negatively, remember that you are not a bad parent.
- Look for autism-friendly film screenings and activities in your area.
- Remember that while there are difficult people about, there are also kind and helpful people out there.
- Use Autism Awareness Cards to let others know why your child is behaving in a certain way and use it as an opportunity to raise autism awareness.

16

The Journey for Parents

It is important to me to say to other parents, you are not alone. We all, at times, feel alone with a special needs child, but we are part of a band of parents and families who need the support of one another and who have a lot to offer one another. Finding ways of connecting and of talking and sharing stories, both sad and funny, helps so much on this journey with autism. My decision to write down everything I have learned through my journey in this book is part of that. I have always kept a personal journal since I was young, and in that sense this book has taken more than ten years to complete as I continued keeping a journal as an adult. Writing a journal has always been my way of giving my feelings an outlet and a place where my deepest fears and thoughts can reside. I want to let others know what my experience has been like and what I've discovered through these years, and in turn I constantly learn from others. I may have been a good doctor before having Brendan, but I am certainly a much better doctor after having Brendan.

Being the parent of a child with autism has been, at times, extremely hard. The last thing I want to do is to give the impression that it might have been easy or that I have effortlessly taken all our difficulties in my stride. There are many times when I have wept, or felt afraid, or deeply anxious, or just hurt by the reactions of others.

I have coped because I had to. I am his mother, I love Brendan and he needed me, so I could not afford to give in, or to feel broken, or to hide my head under the duvet, as I felt like doing on many occasions. And in coping, sometimes well, sometimes not so well, I have built resilience. But I am well aware that for me, as for so many other mothers, fathers and carers out there, it has been a long, tough road and it always will be.

Having Brendan has changed me; I am less driven, a little softer and I have a much better understanding and empathy for parents and carers of special needs children I see at work because I have lived it. In addition to clinical advice, I can offer them practical advice too, based on my own experiences. Parents are often more at ease when I tell them that I too have a child with challenging special needs; it means that we are members of the same 'club' and often I truly understand what they are going through because I went through it.

I don't just give out advice, I take it too. I see lots of children with disabilities as well as those with autism, learning difficulties and other hormonal conditions. I also look after many children with chronic conditions like diabetes, cystic fibrosis and other hormone disorders, and I am truly humbled on a daily basis by the experience of working with them. And plenty of parents give me feedback on things like simple sleep management, diet, schools and how to look at health care plans and educational statements. It is always a two-way street.

I sit on both fences on a daily basis, as a mother to my son with special needs and as a professional who gives advice, care and support to others dealing with children with special needs. And the insight that comes with this makes all the difference in the world. I sometimes hear my well-intentioned colleagues giving words of advice, but until you experience the grief, stress and worries that occur on a daily basis when trying to comfort a child who is anxious, fearful and confused, you can't know just how hard it is to follow some of that advice.

I remember, many times, the feelings of utter helplessness when Brendan rebelled, or had a meltdown or refused to do a task during therapy. I would lose my temper and scold him and then feel utter remorse and shame for the rest of the day. And only a parent of a child with special needs knows that some days you just feel too exhausted or deflated to find that ounce of strength to get through yet another routine or demand. When that happens I think you just have to stop, breathe and let it be. Give yourself a break and try not to feel guilty. Most days are not going to go according to plan or be perfect, but each day we set out, once again, to do our absolute best.

Having Brendan has, in so many ways, been a revelation for me. As someone who has always been highly-motivated, high-achieving and a perfectionist planner, it threw my entire world view to have a child who did not fit in with any of that. I had to let it go and start to see things differently. Not easy, but in the end I am glad. I have learned what it is like to slow everything down, to settle for getting through, rather than coming top, and to take things one small step at a time – especially when sometimes that step is backward, not forward. You can only understand a child by knowing and loving him or her.

Like other parents, I have to remind myself not to wrap my children in bubble-wrap. I want to protect them from being hurt, but I also want to let them discover their strengths and find their place in the world. This is as true for Brendan as it is for my other two children. I want them to have every possible opportunity, to learn new things, to stretch themselves and to feel proud and confident. If I protect Brendan too much then I deny him the opportunity to grow and to learn.

I am very practical and I don't believe in luck. To me you make your 'luck' through hard work and application. I believe that children with ASD need love, guidance, direction and perseverance to help them develop into the best adults that they can become. Success for them can be cultivated with consistent guidance and encouragement. No matter what your child's stage or abilities today, this may change tomorrow. Nothing is set in stone, and ASD children are capable of exceeding predictions and expectations, just as all other children are, as long as we give them the opportunities to develop their skills and abilities.

A few years ago, in 2012 I heard about an autism

conference that was going to be held for the first time at Edge Hill University, minutes from where we were living. And the key speaker was to be Temple Grandin. I had heard about her and read her books, and I was determined to go and hear her speak.

Temple Grandin has autism. And yet she is a professor of animal science at Colorado State University and a best-selling author, speaker and consultant. She has always been an autism advocate and she invented the 'hug machine' to help children and adults with autism to calm down, as well as a machine to de-stress cattle. In 2012, the year of the Edge Hill Conference, she was named as one of Time Magazine's 100 most influential people in the world and in 2017 she was named to the National Women's Hall of Fame in the United States.

At the autism conference Temple spoke about her upbringing. She was born in 1947 and in those days autism was not widely recognised and most people with this kind of special needs were institutionalised. Temple was not put into an institution even though that was what was recommended by the doctors at the time. Her mother, Eustacia, was determined to help her develop her potential and she never gave up on her. Temple said her mother simply would not tolerate bad manners and she insisted that Temple control her meltdowns by taking away the TV for the evening, or in some other way depriving her of something she wanted. Temple said that a child has to be stretched to learn new skills a little at a time and, where possible, given one-to-one teaching from a young age.

I knew the organiser of the autism conference at Edge

Hill, Jude, who arranged for me to have lunch with Temple after she spoke. It was a delight to meet this remarkable woman, so much of what she had said resonated with what I had instinctively felt to be true. Her belief in a disciplined, persistent and ultimately optimistic approach has been my guiding mantra with Brendan.

Temple is very straightforward and practical. After her talk parents would ask questions like, 'How do I stop my child eating so much?' and she would say, 'Put a lock on the fridge,' or 'How can I stop my son taking his clothes off?' Temple's reply was, 'Tell him he can't!'

At lunch she confirmed that she is very definitely someone with autism, she had no social graces or small talk, she ate in silence and she travels with helpers. She was the living embodiment of what is possible for someone who has autism and I was in awe as I sat beside her at the lunch table.

Hearing and meeting Temple Grandin encouraged me greatly. At the time, Brendan was only six, Darren was four and Corinne under one. I was working full-time as a paediatrician, being a wife and mother to three young children and I was navigating my way around the world of autism, looking for ways to help Brendan.

Like so many parents of special needs children I was permanently tired, my nights broken, my days long and demanding. At the same time I was determined to continue working; being a doctor and a paediatrician meant so much to me, I couldn't let my identity as a professional woman disappear. I made difficult choices to take up a consultant post in a district hospital because of the close distance to home instead of travelling far each day if I had taken an academic post in a larger hospital. Despite this, I felt that I should be able to fulfil all my roles, but it took everything I had to do it.

Time and time again I had to dig deep for inner strength. In later years, I was offered managerial and leadership roles at work and I took them; they were the result of many years of hard work and it meant a great deal to me to have achieved this success at work. But at times juggling the demands of work and home has been exhausting.

Things were not always easy for me – at times, like so many other working women, I was undermined and even bullied, and it got me down. But I never let it stop me. Resilience is what we develop in the face of adversity.

At one time I wrote, on a social media platform Twitter, that I was a paediatrician, researcher, mother and wife. I was abused online for not putting mother first in the list! I was stunned – do I have to define myself in order of importance? All aspects of who I am define me and matter deeply to me. I want my children to see their mother working, it sets them, and especially my daughter, an example I want them to follow.

Throughout everything, I have had the love and support of Eugene – a highly talented, meticulous surgeon, a totally committed father and a generous husband. He has stood by me even when he did not agree with my choices and even when it added to his own workload and stress.

Having a special needs child had put our marriage under a lot of strain. We had no time for one another, every minute we were not at work was focussed on Brendan, or the other children and we were often frustrated and taking it out on one another.

There is no such thing as a perfect marriage. I was a teenager who grew up on love story books like Sweet Dreams series and Mills and Boon series and I thought our marriage would be perfect. In Eugene I found someone who loved me wholeheartedly and who showed it; he brought me roses and planned wonderful romantic surprises for my birthdays. But when Brendan came along, after ten years of being just the two of us, the challenges we faced almost broke us apart.

We didn't talk when we should have and, as we realised when we did finally talk, Eugene felt neglected and I felt unsupported. We took the decision to go to marriage counselling after serious consideration, rather than give up on the relationship when the going got really tough, it probably saved our marriage. The use of a mediator or counsellor to resolve deeply entrenched resentments and conflicts proved to be a salvation for us, as we spoke honestly about our feelings and experiences and the impact having Brendan had on our lives. Through counselling we listened to one another, we forgave one another's shortcomings and we reached mutual agreement and compromise.

My parents always believed in me, they were behind me in everything I did. They used to say to me, if you have the heart, you can do it. When I was young, my father created a song about our family's love that he and my mother, my brother and sister and I would sing each night before we went to bed. I have continued this tradition with my children and our own bedtime song of our family's love.

Whatever obstacles and struggles I face, I have my

husband, my children, my parents and my siblings, and that knowledge gives me the strength and courage to face each new day and it makes me feel so grateful.

To other parents I would say this – remember you are not alone, we are all in this together and we can all support one another. And while having a child with autism is one of life's great challenges, it is also one of life's greatest gifts.

Quick Tips

- We can all benefit by sharing information, techniques, ideas and peer support.
- Believe that your child can be stretched to learn new skills, a little at a time.
- Having a special needs child is challenging in a relationship and counselling from an expert can be a great support, for you and your partner.
- You don't always have to be the strong one – let your partner, family and friends support you sometimes.

17

Puberty

When Brendan was ten we moved into our new home. It had been a long time coming – ever since we had seen a piece of land for sale and decided to build our dream house, six years earlier.

We had bought some farmland in Lancashire and knocked down the old cottage on it, which was rundown and too close to the road. We already had a mortgage and there wasn't enough money to build a new home, so we had to go very slowly. But bit by bit we found a way, helped by an architect close friend who was just starting out in practice on her own and who designed it for us for a generous rate.

We wanted it to be an eco-friendly house, using all the sustainable measures possible. It was airtight and relied on ground-source heating, which also heated a small swimming pool. Many of the walls were glass, looking out over the beautiful fields surrounding us which are still part of a local working farm. And we also built an annexe, initially for guests, but eventually we imagined it might give Brendan some independence as he got older while still remaining with us.

The result was a wonderful home which won two Lancashire Design Awards in the residential and sustainability categories.

Each of the children had their own room, but they chose, for the moment, to still remain sleeping in one room together. Brendan slept next to the window to look at the stars, Corinne chose the middle bed and Darren, who was definitely a bookworm, chose the bed next to the books.

The pool meant that they could swim every day. For Brendan this was wonderful – he felt safe and happy in the water and he could exercise daily in a safe and comfortable environment. The three of them would go for a swim when they came home from school almost on a daily basis.

I worried about Brendan becoming addicted to video games on the iPad – he loved them and left to his own devices he would have spent many hours playing games and never interact with anyone. We only ever allowed the children educational and interactive video games, but even these can be pretty compulsive. So we stuck to the system of buying video game time with pasta shells earned through good behaviour and helping with chores and we insisted that he go outside every day as well, to walk Muffin, to ride his bike or to help weed the garden.

Corinne and Darren have busy social lives, especially Corinne, who is very outgoing and sociable. She was always being invited to birthday parties and playdates. I didn't think this bothered Brendan; he had seldom been to birthday parties and when he did go he usually found it overwhelming and spent his time in the corner of the room ignoring everything that was going on. We had held birthday parties for Darren and Corinne and during these parties, Brendan didn't take part in any of the party games and he ignored all the guests and often went into his room to play alone. So I never imagined that he wanted one of his own until one day when I was talking to Darren about his ninth birthday party, Brendan said to me, 'Brendan's birthday party in July'. I was surprised with his statement and I asked him if he wanted his own party and he looked happy and said, 'Yes! Brendan's birthday party!' and named all his friends 'Lewis, Daniel, Tommy, Jack...'

I was puzzled and saddened. I had assumed all this time that Brendan didn't want a party of his own, since he never seemed to enjoy other children's parties, but it seemed I was wrong. He wanted to be like his brother and sister and he wanted his own birthday party, with his own friends. So we gave him a birthday party, his very first, for his eleventh birthday. Brendan wrote down the names of all eight of his classmates on his own, all of them had autism, and we invited them to our house.

The parents of the other children were delighted. They all told us that their children had never been invited to a birthday party before and my heart ached, as this was true for Brendan too, apart from one party when he was at nursery.

Six of the eight in his class came, with their parents. We made it a swimming party, with a big cake and food for the children and adults. I had to check with each family

154

what their child could eat. Luckily they all liked nuggets and chips, which helped.

Brendan was very excited before the party and he managed it so well – no disappearing to his room, he was in the pool splashing about with his own friends and they ate together afterwards. All the parents were so happy about it and the children seemed to genuinely enjoy it.

Over the following year we could see that Brendan was approaching puberty. Eleven and a half is the average age for the onset of puberty in boys, and Brendan was spot-on. As a paediatric endocrinologist I am pretty familiar with puberty and I knew that Brendan had started his as soon as we began to notice his body odour. That distinctive, sour smell may be the first sign that your child's hormones are on the rampage and their body is undergoing a transformation.

What I wasn't prepared for was the aggression, the anxieties and mood swings and the spontaneous erections and masturbation. Even in children who do not have autism puberty can be a difficult transition due to hormonal changes and mood swings are common, but for a child with autism, who can't understand what is going on, it can be so much harder.

Brendan's emotional outbursts got a lot worse during this time and my patience was often tested. His self-harming behaviours, pinching and biting himself, also escalated. To help him cope with this we used a lot of the PECS cards to show him what was happening. We also use a traffic light system at home that was first introduced to us at Brendan's autism school.

The traffic light system is specifically for addressing

problem behaviours. The child can earn privileges at different levels, corresponding to the green, yellow and red of the traffic lights. If the child earns green it means they are behaving well and they are rewarded with the highest level of privileges. Yellow is the intermediate level, when the child might still be engaging in minor problem behaviours but generally trying and making progress. Red indicates that the child is still engaging in severe problem behaviours, such as showing aggression or having frequent meltdowns.

The good thing about the traffic light system is that it isn't all or nothing – the child can move between colours according to how they are behaving throughout the day.

The goal of the system is to motivate the child to control his or her own behaviour in order to earn rewards and privileges. The focus is not on punishment, but rather reinforcing the child's positive view of himself for behaving appropriately by offering lots of rewards and encouragement.

The traffic light system helped with managing Brendan through this tough time – he could move from red to yellow fairly quickly and he understood how it worked. But there were also times when we needed to let him do whatever worked for him – such as playing his favourite Minecraft video game – to distract him from outbursts of aggression that he could not manage to contain.

We taught him to have daily baths and showers and to use deodorant to keep himself clean and fresh-smelling. We created step-by-step PECS visuals of which parts of his body he needed to pay special attention to in the bath or shower.

There was very little point at this stage to try to discuss

sexuality with Brendan because he would not comprehend it, and yet it was important to lay out some ground rules. He would sometimes put his hands down his trousers while we were in public, so we had to teach him the difference between being in public and in private and that some things could only happen in private. Masturbation was only for the bedroom and not anywhere else.

We also needed to teach him about safety; that he should not let anyone touch his private parts, that he should never touch anyone else's and that he should tell us if anything like this ever happened. All of this was difficult to teach to a child with special needs, involving completely new concepts for him, and it took several months of daily work and visual aids. But he got there and he understood.

By the time he turned 12, in 2016, we were very proud of his achievements. Brendan could manage himself in all kinds of situations, he could cope with change, he was in a nurturing school where he had friends, he could manage all his basic routines, from teeth-cleaning to showers to making his bed, and he could eat a meal on his own, do his homework or carry out his chores without fuss.

Academically he had reached the capabilities of a child of seven or eight. He could do a jigsaw of 50 pieces (gradually increased, over the years, from five), he was quite good at reading, writing and spelling and he loved National Geographic Kids magazine.

In terms of speech Brendan could tell us what he wanted (for instance the birthday party or toys for Christmas) but he hadn't yet progressed to meaningful conversations – that became our next goal. He would often repeat words or phrases that he had heard from advertisements, films or other people. This form of mimicry is a term called 'echolalia' which is often present in people with autism. It can make no sense to someone who doesn't understand Brendan. If for example he is asked what he wants to eat for lunch, Brendan may well respond with a phrase he likes to repeat 'Compare dot com!' (an advertisement quote he often hears and repeats from the TV).

Echolalia can be immediate or delayed. Immediate echolalia is repetition immediately after something is heard. For example when I ask Brendan to 'Sit down on the chair', he may immediately respond with 'On the chair!' Delayed echolalia is when the child has heard something and repeats it at a later time. Both types of echolalia may be a form of interaction for the child with autism. It may just buy them time as they try to process what was being said and how to respond, or it may be their way of trying to engage in a conversation when they do not have the capacity to create new words or responses.

Another challenging behaviour for children with autism is speaking in an abnormal tone, pitch or rhythm. Brendan developed a habit of talking very loudly, to the point of shouting, at times. This could often startle a lot of people when we were in public and I had to apologise, repeatedly, to many strangers. Children with autism often don't realise that they are talking far too loudly and will not understand why talking in a loud voice isn't always socially appropriate. Neither will they understand that changing the volume of their own voice communicates different messages to others. I have often had to show Brendan a

PECS picture of voice volume control or a hand signal, to show him that he is talking too loudly and to get him to reduce his voice to a 'speaking voice'.

Over the years Brendan has become technologically competent and this brought him a lot of joy. He loved to make figures out of Lego and when he was about nine he put together a Lego helicopter, which subsequently was accidentally broken apart. I had not kept the instructions booklet and I was worried about how he would rebuild it, until I saw Brendan looking up the instructions on the computer through Google. It was lovely for us to see him work out for himself what he needed to do, and simply go ahead and do it.

Brendan's maths is not wonderful, it took him a long time to learn to add and subtract and he is still learning to manage multiplication and division. One of the most important skills to teach children with autism is money maths as this is an essential part of independent living in the future. Brendan's school concentrated on areas like this; the kind of skills that would enable the children to have a degree of independence as adults. From Year Three Brendan had weekly trips with the school to go shopping in a supermarket – they would be given a shopping list of items to buy and had to work out the prices and manage their money to pay for their purchases at the supermarket.

Many people wrongly believe that everyone with autism is a savant; which is someone with a highly exceptional ability in a specific area, such as maths, music, memory or art. The film Rain Man brought savants into public focus, when Dustin Hoffman played a man with autism, able to memorise entire phone books. Other savants, such as architectural artist Stephen Wiltshire, have also attracted a lot of publicity. But while the occurrence of savants is higher among those with autism – about ten percent as opposed to one percent in the population as a whole – that still means that most people with autism are not savants. The majority of people with autism have different levels of learning or behavioural difficulties.

While Brendan's capability with technology did outstrip his ability in other areas, rather than being exceptional it was closer to the norm for a very bright and able boy of his age, with or without autism.

Brendan is now in his teens, and he is still learning and expanding in his capabilities every day. Brendan is still far from neurotypical or normal to the rest of the world. He still has his stimming behaviours, loud noises and severe anxieties. He often finds it hard to find his own speech to communicate. But he is definitely his own person who triumphs over each challenge and he enjoys playing on the video games, iPad and watching his favourite Disney shows.

Every school term, we contribute to his Individual Educational Plan or I.E.P to ensure that he makes progress and that both the school and home environments are on par with the goals and targets. The I.E.Ps provide us with an opportunity to sit down and communicate with his teachers to develop a plan to try and improve Brendan's learning or behavioural goals. We have never missed any of his annual review meetings to discuss and review his EHCP, which are attended by the Special Educational Needs and Disability (SEND) Officer from the local authority and the school representative, usually the teacher. These yearly meetings can often be emotional and challenging for parents who continue to fight to ensure that their child gets the support he or she needs. The effectiveness of the support provided should then be reviewed on a regular basis. While Brendan clearly has limitations both behaviourally and cognitively and he will never fully fit in with the social norms of society, he has come such a long way, and I believe he still has a long way to go.

Quick Tips

- Your child will never stop surprising you. So keep listening to them and encouraging them.
- Echolalia, whether it is immediate or delayed, can be a form of interaction for the person with autism.
- Use picture cards or PECS to teach your child to control the volume of his or her voice. Demonstrate the volume of voice to use when talking to you. Pretend play can give opportunities to act out different social situations and practice varying voice levels in different situations.
- Puberty brings a raft of new challenges, so make sure you are fully prepared.
- Use a currency system so that your child can earn points for chores that can be spent on video game or screen time. Teach your child basic household chores and insist they are done regularly.
- Use the traffic light system or any other individualised system that works.

to control his or her own behaviour in order to earn rewards and privileges.

- Always be involved in your child's I.E.P. at school and attend the school annual review meetings to ensure your voice and your views are heard.
- Be prepared and read the last I.E.P. plan to review what was achieved. Try and find out what your child's needs or any unmet needs are. Has their behavioural goals been achieved?
- Make a list of accomplishments, concerns and what are the current challenges.
- What can you do at home to support the agreed goals and at the end of the meeting, how will both you and the school measure progress?

18

Into the Future

Autism is a spectrum and it can change its colours, shapes and forms as your child grows. I have learned that by loving Brendan, observing him day to day and using trial and error methods to constantly push the boundaries of what he can do, I grow to understand him and his way of seeing the world a little better each day.

So much of what I read in Naoki Higashida's book, 'The Reason I Jump' and subsequently in his second book, 'Fall Down 7 Times, Get Up 8' has been a true reflection of Brendan over the years. Naoki has proven to us that lack of speech is certainly not a reflection of lack of intelligence.

Language is a medium to connect with one another and to be denied this form of communication is to limit the child to frustration, loneliness, anger and fear. Imagine Stephen Hawking's life without his computer as a means of communicating with the world!

As a mother of two sons who were non-verbal, I have spent years trying to recognise their abilities and their need to communicate. Darren was diagnosed with congenital deafness late and he spent his early educational years in a speech and language special needs school learning sign language, and then learning to 'hear' again after his diagnosis, once he had hearing aids. I had initially been told that he had learning difficulties and that he was performing below par in all academic areas; reading, speaking and writing. Today, at 11 years old Darren is a top student every year in a mainstream school.

Similarly, with Brendan, we felt it was our duty to provide him with a means of communication and we never gave up because I knew in my heart that Brendan was trying to speak but just couldn't find the words. Before he could speak Brendan was still able to communicate through his PECS cards and Liberator AAC device. This reduced a lot of the frustrations and frequency of meltdowns. Many famous non-verbal people with autism like Naoki Higashida and Tito Mukhopadhyay communicate by typing or using a letter board and they have proven to the world that lack of speech need not equate to lack of communication. I hope that the growing awareness and understanding of autism means that it will never be assumed that lack of speech is a lack of intelligence or ability.

I have also realised it is a myth that those with autism do not want to be included and feel no empathy. I have seen Brendan upset because either Darren or Corinne is upset, I have seen him yearning for a birthday party of his own, I have seen him playing with his siblings and friends. He may not be able to express all that he feels, but I can see the love he has for them.

The most important thing we can give him is love, patience and consistency, every day in every possible way. With inconsistency Brendan grows anxious, confused and upset. So we aim for consistency most of the time. When we bring someone into his life – an au pair, a new teacher – we have to show them how to maintain his routines and expectations without disruption. With his routines in place he is happy, he knows the world around him and he is free from fear.

For us his growing years are a journey that is still, at times, fraught with uncertainty and new challenges. As his mother, acceptance that autism is a part of Brendan was a process that grew and I clearly remember the cycles of grief, denial, anger, depression and bargaining, but at the heart of it all was my love for him. He is my son.

We watch Brendan and we learn about him all the time, as he interacts with his brother, his sister and Muffin. We don't always get it right around him, there are many times we have got it wrong, but we keep on trying.

As for the future, it is an unknown, but we do have hopes and dreams for him. We would like to see him able to live independently as a young adult, with a job and an income. We think often about what kind of job he might be able to do. We want his life to have a sense of meaning and purpose and I believe work is a key part of this.

The National Autistic Society reports that only 16 percent of adults with autism are in full-time paid work. Even among those who take degrees and graduate, there is an unemployment level of 26 percent – the largest proportion of any disability group. In addition, when adults with autism do work there are often difficulties – around a third have experienced bullying, unfair treatment or discrimination from co-workers or employers.

These reports are worrying for any parent of a child with autism. But we have to keep on pushing the boundaries and working to improve the prospects for those with autism.

It is possible to create more inclusive workplaces and to find employers willing to meet this challenge.

One of my greatest ambitions for the future is to set up a local social enterprise for autism like Café Autisan. This is a wonderful project, set up by the National Autistic Society. The cafe is in Whalley Abbey in Lancashire, it was set up as part of a wider enterprise initiative, and adults with autism are employed in the cafe, preparing and selling tea and coffee, cakes and sandwiches. Working in the cafe they are able to complete an NVQ (National Vocational Qualification) in catering and hospitality, as well as other workplace-based qualifications which will greatly enhance their employment prospects.

I hope this enterprise will become a reality in the area where we live and eventually across the country, offering real work prospects for those with autism. There are already similar initiatives in several locations around the country, including Southport and Sussex. These initiatives offer real hope of meaningful employment for those with autism.

Because we don't know what Brendan's future holds, we have set up a Living Disability Trust Fund or also known as Trust for Disabled and Vulnerable People. We sought advice from professionals and we were made aware that it will probably not be in a vulnerable or disabled person's interest if they were to receive an inheritance from us directly. Additionally, the beneficiary may not be in a position themselves to manage any inheritance. A Trust Fund is a useful way to provide financial stability for a disabled or vulnerable person throughout their lifetime. At the moment Eugene and I are the trustees, but when they are grown up Darren and Corinne will become the trustees, in charge of their brother's welfare so that his needs will be taken care of. They will know him and love him better than anyone else in the world.

When a special needs child turns 18 they become the ward of the state and the parents have to name themselves as the child's guardian or they may lose the right to influence the care of their child. Although most local authorities do take the parents' wishes into account, under law they do not have to. So we will be Brendan's guardians.

As a researcher, I am grateful that autism research and funding has changed our understanding of this social learning disability and that there are now driving advances in early diagnosis, evidence-based interventions and, ultimately, better outcomes.

Brendan changed my view of the world and taught me about life and living. Without him I would have been a 'tiger mum' pushing my children to succeed. Now I want them to feel loved and happy above all else. I want them to be kind and patient and understanding, to care about the world and about their fellow human beings.

My hope is that awareness of autism will grow, along with education, social programmes, employment initiatives and opportunities for those with ASD and special needs.

And my hope for Brendan is that he will always find acceptance and understanding wherever he goes, and that he will always know how much he is loved.

Only time will tell…

Time

By Darren Toh, Age 8

Time is…
An unknown force surrounding the universe,
A curious person putting his nose into everything,
And a great vision of a four dimensional world.

Time is…
Something that will never stop in any situation,
One of the beautiful things that meets the eye,
And a type of food that flavours your taste buds.

Time is…
Part of the spirit of God when he died,
A kind of gas escaping from being discovered,
And a magic spell wandering alone.

Time is…
A friendly animal wanting to play with you,
An explorer scouring the world, looking for whatever may be hiding,

And the sunset at the end of the day.

Time is…
Fascinating,
It follows us each day.
It's here, there and everywhere,
It's just its special way.

Time is…
Immortal,
It is immortal just like gods.
Time always tells the time,
With things that we call clocks.

Time…
Began with the big bang,
It happened deep in space.
I think now we all agree,
That time is a wonderful place.

19

Further Information

<u>Diagnosing Autistic Spectrum Disorder</u>

If you think your child may have autism, begin keeping a diary of your child's behaviours and symptoms. It can be useful to compare these to a list of standard developmental milestones.

If you have concerns your health visitor or GP, many carry out a screening called M-CHAT (Modified Checklist for Autism in Toddlers) or ADOS (Autism Diagnostic Observation Schedule). This is not a diagnosis, but may indicate that it is worthwhile taking your child for a multi-disciplinary diagnostic assessment.

The signs that a child may have ASD can include:

- Repetitive behaviours
- Not pointing at objects
- Ignoring things that are happening nearby
- Difficulty with social interaction and communication
- Biting, pinching, kicking or self-injuring

For more details about the signs of autism and sources of help, visit the website of the National Autistic Society at www.autism.org.uk

Chapter 1

To find a private speech therapist in your area visit the Association of Speech and Language Therapists at:

www.helpwithtalking.com

This website provides information and a contact point for members of the public searching for private Speech and Language Therapists. Access to NHS speech therapists requires a referral from the GP, health visitor or paediatrician.

Chapter 6

https://www.eric.org.uk/Pages/Category/bedwetting

This website provides further information on the common childhood bowel and bladder problems and where you can get help and support for your child.

Chapter 8

Visit The Hanen Centre website for details of all their activities, including specific courses:

www.hanen.org

It Takes Two- is a program designed specifically for parents of young children (birth to 5 years of age) who have been identified as having a language delay and helps adjust everyday routines to help your child take turns and keep interactions going
http://www.hanen.org/Programs/For-Parents/It-Takes-Two-to-Talk.aspx

More Than Words-is a program designed specifically for parents of children ages 5 and under on the autism spectrum and with other social communication difficulties. It addresses the unique needs of these children and provides parents with the tools, strategies and support to improve communications and social skills
http://www.hanen.org/Programs/For-Parents/More-Than-Words.aspx

EarlyBird Programmes

EarlyBird (under five years) and EarlyBird Plus (ages four-nine) are support programmes for parents and carers, offering advice and guidance on strategies and approaches for dealing with young autistic children. Both programmes work on understanding autism, building confidence to encourage interaction and communication, and understanding and supporting behaviour.
The EarlyBird programmes are run by the National Autistic Society and you can find details of these on their website:
https://www.autism.org.uk/services/community/family-support/earlybird.aspx

British Signalong

You can find details of the Signalong courses on the website for Signalong, the British Communication Charity:

www.signalong.org.uk

Mr Tumble

The Something Special series was produced by CBeebies from 2004 to 2014 and was presented by Justin Fletcher with Mr Tumble, using Makaton. Aimed at special needs children, the shows were colourful and fun and you can still find them on the BBC.

Makaton

For details of the Makaton language programme visit the Makaton website:

www.makaton.org

TEACCH

For details of the TEACCH Autism Programme visit:

www.teacch.com

Applied Behaviour Analysis

For details of this approach visit:

www.autismspeaks.org

You can also find details on this very useful website:

www.educateautism.com

Chapter 9

To find out more about the Picture Exchange Communication System (PECS) visit:

www.pecsunitedkingdom.com

The Advisory Centre for Education (ACE) provides free advice to parents on all aspects of state-funded education for special needs children:

www.ace-ed.org.uk

To find out more about the Liberator electronic voice output device visit:

www.liberator.co.uk
www.asha.org/public/speech/disorders/AAC/

The International Society for Augmentative and Alternative Communication (ISAAC) works to improve the lives of children and adults with complex communication needs:

www.isaac-online.org

Proloquo2Go is an award-winning symbol-supported communication app. It provides a voice to over 150,000 individuals who cannot speak.

www.assistiveware.com/product/proloquo2go

Chapter 10

For a useful starting place with finding forums for the
parents and families of children with autism, try the
following websites:
Autism UK Independent runs chat forums on all kinds of
aspects of autism:

www.autismuk.com

Ambitious About Autism is the UK's largest online autism
community:

www.ambitiousaboutautism.co.uk

ASD Friendly (Available Supportive Devoted Friendly) is for
parents and carers sharing their experience of everyday
life with children with autism. There are others available
day and night to talk:

www.asdfriendly.org

Chapter 11

For advice about applying for an Education, Health and
Care Plan (EHCP) visit The National Autistic Society
at:

https://www.autism.org.uk/about/in-education/extra-help-in-school/england/ehc-plans.aspx

This will give clear and useful advice about the EHCP and about funding. Only a local authority can carry out an EHC needs assessment. Child Autism UK advise on, provide training for and supply ABA (Applied Behavioural Analysis) tutors and services.

www.childautism.co.uk

Parent Partnership can be fantastically useful and supportive.

https://www.pacey.org.uk/working-in-childcare/spotlight-on/partnerships-with-parents/

Consult the Council for Disabled Children for your local Information Advice and Support Services Network

www.councilfordisabledchildren.org.uk

You can also look at the National Portage Association for information about portage and home visiting educational services for pre-school children with special educational needs:

www.portage.org.uk

Other sites to check out as a resource for autism advice, support and available services are:

www.helpwithautism.co.uk
www.ambitiousaboutautism.org.uk
www.autism-alliance.org.uk
www.autismtoolbox.co.uk

Here are some general guidelines about the types of school available:

<u>Applying for a Place at School</u>

Your local authority (LA) only has a duty to provide an 'adequate' education for your child – it does not have to provide the best education. However, they are obliged to offer you information about schools which are available locally and to explain their decision about where they wish to place your child.

Some schools may have autism accreditation, a quality assurance programme that some services, like schools, choose to be a part of.

The following types of schools are available (although not all these types of school will necessarily be available in your local area).

- Mainstream schools: some children with autism are educated in mainstream primary and secondary schools. If your child has an Education, Health and Care Plan (EHCP), they may have extra support in school for a set number of hours a week. It is unlawful under the Disability Discrimination Act 1995 (as amended by the Special Educational Needs Disability Act 2001) for schools in England and Wales to discriminate against children or young people with a disability with regard to admissions, education and associated services, and exclusions.

- A base or unit within a mainstream school: some mainstream primary and secondary schools have classes for pupils with ASD within them. The pupils access the mainstream school when appropriate and are educated in the base or unit for the rest of the time.
- Special schools: these are schools specifically for children with special educational needs. The pupils they cater for vary: some are just for pupils with ASD while others are for pupils with moderate or severe learning difficulties, pupils with physical difficulties, or a mixture of the two.
- Residential schools: these schools can be for children with varying needs or specific needs. Pupils stay overnight and have a 24-hour curriculum – meaning there is support available 24 hours a day. Some have a 52-week placement, others go home at weekends or during the holidays. A multi-agency plan should be put into place that establishes joint or tripartite funding, but it remains the responsibility of the local authority to ensure that every child has an education. Parents and local authorities should agree any arrangements for

a pupil's contact with their family and for any special help, such as transport.

- Independent or non-maintained schools: these schools can be mainstream, special or residential, but none of them will be maintained by the local authority. Parents can choose to place their child at their own expense or to make representation to their local authority for a placement at an independent or non-maintained school.

You don't need to visit every school you hear about (and it would not be possible anyway) but it's a good idea to visit as many different types of school as possible. This will give you a better idea of what is available and which features you think are important. You may find that a type of school you wouldn't have considered could, in fact, be right for your child. For example, one parent was told by her son's educational psychologist that he would not be able to cope in a mainstream school. However, when she visited her local primary school she decided that it was actually suitable because it was quite small and had a very calm and caring ethos.

You may not think that some schools are suitable for your child, but find that they still have elements that appeal to you. For example, a speech and language therapy unit in a mainstream school might not suit your child, but the fact that the children there spend a lot of time in mainstream classes could be something that they would benefit from. As a result, you might choose to look at the arrangements that are made for inclusion of pupils with disabilities in mainstream classes at the other schools you visit.

Always remember that you are your child's advocate. No-one believes in your child's ability as much as you do. Trust your gut feeling and don't be afraid to write letters to request and argue for what you believe is the right placement for your child.

Template letter requesting a statutory educational assessment:

Dear Sir/Madam,

Child's name and date of birth

I am writing as the parent of the above child to request an assessment of his/her special educational needs under section 323 of the 1996 Education Act. [Insert child's name] attends [insert name of school/ early years setting].

I believe that my child needs more help than the school/setting is able to provide. His/her special educational needs are as follows:

[Here you could outline the difficulties your child is having at school/setting and at home, send information about any diagnosis, outline any support your child has been receiving and who (if anyone) outside the school/setting has been involved]

My reasons for believing that the school cannot on their own make the provision required to meet my child's needs are:

[Here you could outline your continuing concerns about your child's progress in relation to peers, any increased behavioural difficulties, progress through an Action or Action Plus programme, etc]
I would like you to seek advice from the following people, who are involved with my child.

[List the people involved, giving addresses where necessary]

I understand that you are required by law to reply to this request within six weeks and that if you refuse to carry out an assessment, I will be able to appeal to a tribunal.

Yours sincerely

Chapter 12

Great children's websites for digital learning:

www.busythings.co.uk
www.starfall.com
https://www.twinkl.co.uk/

Chapter 13

The Nuffield Dyspraxia Programme (NDP) is primarily for three to seven year-olds and it provides a comprehensive treatment package including therapy principles and techniques and picture resources to treat developmental verbal dyspraxia, childhood apraxia of speech and other severe speech disorders.

www.ndp3.org

Find out more about social stories through the National Autistic Society at:

http://www.autism.org.uk/professionals/teachers/ myworldhub/socialstories.aspx

Twinkl had a wide range of resources for social stories, including worksheets, PowerPoints and games:

www.twinkl.co.uk

Educate Autism also has useful information and resources on social stories (as well as plenty else, including a variety of tools to help with teaching children with autism):

www.educateautism.com

Chapter 14

Support dogs is an organisation that trains autism assistance dogs. However they can only provide dogs within a two-hour catchment area from Sheffield, where they are based:

www.supportdogs.org.uk

Autism Life Dogs provide trained autism support dogs or will consider bespoke training for your family dog:

www.autismlifedogs.com

You can also contact Dogs for Good which provides assistance and support dogs for conditions including autism:

www.dogsforgood.org

Paws with a Cause is another helpful organisation which provides assistance dogs for those with a variety of conditions, including autism:

www.pawswithacause.org

Chapter 15

Dimensions provides research-based, outcomes-focussed support services for people with learning disabilities and autism. Alongside supported living and residential care, they also offer specialist services including Positive Behaviour Support and useful information including autism-friendly cinema screenings:

www.dimensions-uk.org

For Autism Awareness Cards go to the National Autistic Society.

You can also find them at the following :

https://community.autism.org.uk/f/health-and-wellbeing/15498/autism-awareness-alert-cards

Other courses

The Son-Rise Program based in the USA is an educational treatment modality is based on the principles of deep acceptance of the child and the autism. It encourages joining, rather than stopping, a child's repetitive, exclusive and ritualistic behaviors. By doing so, it builds rapport and connection, and motivation for the child to learn and progress.

https://autismtreatmentcenter.org/

Intensive interaction program is an approach to help people with learning difficulties or autism at the early stages of development and works on early interaction abilities such as eye contact, facial expressions and vocalisations.

https://www.intensiveinteraction.org/

Books

There are many books on autism available, but the ones I have found most useful are:

The Reason I Jump by Naoki Higashida and David Mitchell is widely available. Naoki and David's latest book released in 2017 is *Fall Down 7 Times Get Up 8*. Naoki is now in his twenties and this is another wonderful insight into his world.

Temple Grandin's books, all of which are available include:
The Autistic Brain (written with Ricanek)
Thinking in Pictures
The Loving Push: How Parents and Professionals Can Help Spectrum Kids Become Successful Adults (written with Debra Moore)

Author Biography

Dr May Ng, *MBBS (Hons) FRCPCH FHEA MSc LLM MBA PhD* is an Honorary Associate Professor at the University of Liverpool and holds a dual accreditation for specialist qualifications in General Paediatrics and Paediatric Endocrinology and Diabetes. She qualified in medicine at University of Sydney, Australia before training in paediatrics in Australia and later in

United Kingdom. Dr Ng completed a Master's degree in Medical Science in 2005 and was awarded a UK Medical Research Council Fellowship grant in 2006, subsequently completing her doctoral PhD thesis in paediatric endocrinology and diabetes. Dr Ng also completed a Master in Laws degree and a MBA whilst working full-time and she is active in medicolegal work. She has produced over 200 scientific papers, including three Cochrane systematic reviews, and has presented at more than 300 scientific meetings internationally. She serves on the editorial board for several international journals including as Editor-in-Chief and Associate Editor. Dr Ng has been a keynote speaker at many international meetings of learned societies including Diabetes UK/Ireland, Sri Lanka, Malaysia, Diabetes Professional Conference, National Network Forums and Royal Colleges. She is actively involved in the development of national paediatric training and policies in endocrine and diabetes, and she and her team have won several national awards, including:

University of Liverpool Alumni Award 2020, HSJ Diabetes Initiative Finalist 2019, Diabetes UK Mary Mackinnon Award 2018, Diabetes Quality in Care (QiC) Team of the Year 2017 finalist, Asian Women of Achievement Award UK 2016 finalist, UK 2015 Diabetes Quality in Care (QiC) Winner, Highly Commended British Medical Journal Diabetes Team of the Year 2015 and Finalist HSJ Clinical Leader of the Year 2015.

Dr May Ng also serves as Chair of the UK Association of Children's Diabetes Clinicians, UK Training Advisor for paediatric endocrinology and diabetes specialty training at the Royal College of Paediatrics, Online Learning Committee for European Society of Paediatric Endocrinology, and Guidelines Officer for the British Society of Paediatric Endocrinology and Diabetes. She is a member of the External Reference Group for the National Institute of Clinical Excellence and the National Steering Group for Children and Young People's Diabetes Peer Review.

She lives in Lancashire and is married with three children and a dog. She enjoys reading, dog-walking and is regularly involved in the promotion of Autism and Deaf Awareness.

Twitter @mayng888
Website: www.paedsdoc.co.uk